OXFORD

Mastermaths 1

Paul Briten

1

1999 002

Oxford University Press

Oxford University Press, Great Clarendon Street, Oxford OX2 6DP

Oxford New York
Athens Auckland Bangkok Bogota Bombay
Buenos Aires Calcutta Cape Town Dar es Salaam
Delhi Florence Hong Kong Istanbul Karachi
Kuala Lumpur Madras Madrid Melbourne
Mexico City Nairobi Paris Singapore
Taipei Tokyo Toronto Warsaw

and associated companies in
Berlin Ibadan

Oxford is a trade mark of Oxford University Press

© Paul Briten 1997

First published 1984
Reprinted 1985, 1989, 1991, 1993, 1994 (twice)
New Edition 1997

ISBN 0 19 834837 1

Typeset by Tradespools Ltd, Frome and Hardlines, Charlbury

Illustrated by CGS Studios, Cheltenham

Printed in Hong Kong

Contents

Contents

Assessment questions – key to levels:
black = level 2 or below; red = level 3; black in red circle = level 4

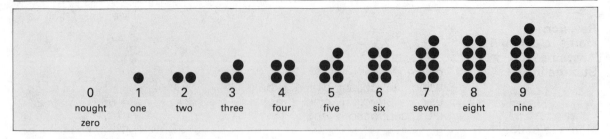

0	1	2	3	4	5	6	7	8	9
nought zero	one	two	three	four	five	six	seven	eight	nine

A How many men in each boat?

☆ 3

1
2
3
4

5
6
7
8

B How many boats?

☆ three

1
2
3
4
5

C How many dots?

☆ 6

1
2
3
4

5
6
7
8

D Draw a line of:

☆ 9 dots

1 4 dots	5 3 dots
2 2 dots	6 8 dots
3 7 dots	7 1 dot
4 5 dots	8 6 dots

E How many:

☆ pink fish? 4

| 1 white fish? | 3 black fish? |
| 2 red fish? | |

Numbers to 9

0	1	2	3	4	5	6	7	8	9
nought zero	one	two	three	four	five	six	seven	eight	nine

counting on ⟶   ⟵ **counting back**

A Copy and complete:

☆ 0 ✱ ✱ 3 ✱ ✱ 6
   0 1 2 3 4 5 6

1   0 ✱ 2 ✱ 4 ✱ 6
2   3 ✱ 5 ✱ ✱ 8 9
3   2 ✱ ✱ 5 ✱ ✱ 8
4   4 ✱ ✱ ✱ 8 ✱
5   ✱ ✱ 2 ✱ ✱ ✱ 6
6   1 ✱ ✱ ✱ ✱ ✱ 7

B Write these numbers in order, **smallest first**:

☆ 3 7 1 8 9
  1 3 7 8 9

1   6 1 3 5 4
2   7 2 8 3 9
3   6 3 0 5 4
4   1 3 7 0 5
5   9 5 3 8 1 2
6   4 8 6 1 7 0

C Write the number that is **one more than**:

☆ three   4

1 six   4 two   7 five
2 four   5 one   8 zero
3 eight   6 seven

D Copy and complete:

☆ 8 ✱ ✱ ✱ 4 ✱ ✱
   8 7 6 5 4 3 2

1   9 ✱ 7 ✱ ✱ ✱ 3
2   7 ✱ ✱ 4 ✱ ✱ 1
3   9 ✱ ✱ 6 ✱ ✱ ✱
4   8 ✱ ✱ 5 ✱ ✱ ✱
5   ✱ ✱ 4 ✱ ✱ 1 ✱
6   ✱ 5 ✱ ✱ ✱ ✱ 0

E Write these numbers in order, **largest first**:

☆ 4 7 3 9 1
  9 7 4 3 1

1   7 5 9 6 8
2   2 7 9 4 5
3   3 2 6 4 8
4   6 3 5 0 7
5   1 4 0 9 6 3
6   8 3 0 5 9 1

F Write the number that is **one less than**:

☆ seven   6

1 nine   4 two   7 one
2 three   5 eight   8 six
3 four   6 five

How many counters altogether?

Write:　**5　+　3　=　8**
Say:　'five add three equals eight'

How many counters altogether?

four add three equals seven
4　+　3　=　7

A How many counters altogether:

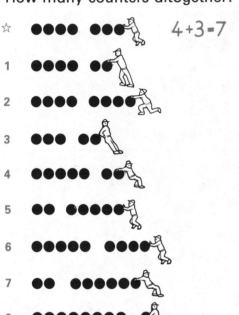

☆　　4+3=7

1

2

3

4

5

6

7

8

9

10

B Use counters if you need to.
Write numbers for ✳'s:

☆ 4+1=✳ 5

1　3+1=✳　　　8　1+7=✳
2　2+2=✳　　　9　3+3=✳
3　1+6=✳　　　10　4+4=✳
4　6+3=✳　　　11　3+2=✳
5　3+4=✳　　　12　2+3=✳
6　5+4=✳　　　13　5+2=✳
7　8+1=✳　　　14　2+5=✳

C Write in **figures** and **signs**:

☆ three add two equals five

3+2=5

1 two add four equals six
2 five add one equals six
3 four add two equals six
4 seven add one equals eight
5 two add six equals eight
6 eight add nought equals eight
7 three add six equals nine
8 six add three equals nine

D Write numbers for ✳'s:

☆ six add two equals ✳ 8
1 five add three equals ✳
2 one add seven equals ✳
3 three add three equals ✳
4 four add nought equals ✳
5 two add six equals ✳
6 five add four equals ✳
7 four add five equals ✳
8 four add four equals ✳

E Write numbers for ✳'s:

☆ 6+3=✳ 9
1 4+3=✳　　　6 1+1=✳
2 2+4=✳　　　7 6+0=✳
3 1+4=✳　　　8 5+4=✳
4 0+4=✳　　　9 0+3=✳
5 2+2=✳　　　10 1+8=✳

Numbers to 9

5+3=8
3+5=8

> The sign < means **is less than**
> The sign > means **is greater than**
>
> 4 < 9 means '4 is less than 9'
> 6+2 > 5 means '6+2 is greater than 5'
>   or   **8 is greater than 5**

A Use counters if you need to.
Write numbers for ✱'s:

☆ 4+2=✱   6
  2+4=✱   6

1 6+1=✱   6 4+3=✱
   1+6=✱   3+4=✱
2 5+4=✱   7 2+6=✱
   4+5=✱   6+2=✱
3 7+2=✱   8 3+0=✱
   2+7=✱   0+3=✱
4 4+0=✱   9 5+2=✱
   0+4=✱   2+5=✱
5 3+2=✱   10 8+1=✱
   2+3=✱   1+8=✱

B Write numbers for ✱'s:

☆ 6+✱=9   3

1 4+3=✱   9 9+0=✱
2 3+✱=7   10 0+✱=9
3 2+6=✱   11 1+7=✱
4 6+✱=8   12 ✱+1=8
5 7+✱=9   13 6+3=✱
6 ✱+7=9   14 3+✱=9
7 3+2=✱   15 3+✱=8
8 2+✱=5   16 5+✱=8

C Write the sign < or > for ✱'s:

☆ 7✱5   >

1 3✱6   9 6✱9
2 9✱4   10 6✱4
3 8✱3   11 5✱6
4 0✱1   12 1✱8
5 7✱5   13 6✱5
6 4✱2   14 1✱7
7 7✱8   15 0✱9
8 2✱4   16 8✱2

D Write the sign < or > for ✱'s:

☆ 6✱5+2   <

1 3+1✱6   11 5✱4+2
2 2+5✱9   12 6✱5+4
3 4+4✱7   13 9✱6+2
4 3+5✱7   14 2✱4+2
5 8+1✱2   15 0✱4+0
6 0+5✱7   16 7✱6+3
7 4+5✱3   17 3✱4+3
8 6+2✱9   18 1✱3+3
9 2+2✱1   19 4✱2+3
10 1+6✱8   20 8✱5+4

is greater than

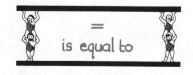

is equal to

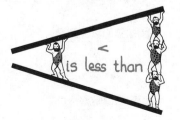

is less than

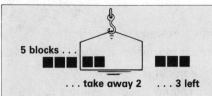

5 blocks . . .

. . . take away 2   . . . 3 left

You can use subtraction to take away.
Write: 5−2=3

Take away **4** counters from this group:

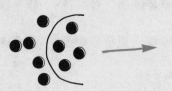

How many are left? **5**
Write: 9−4=5

A Write how many are left:

☆ 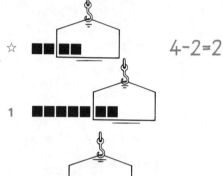   4-2=2

1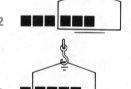

2

3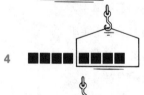

4

5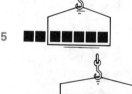

6

7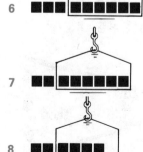

8

B How many counters are left if you:

☆ take away 3?

   7-3=4

1 take away 2?	6 take away 2?
2 take away 4?	7 take away 4?
3 take away 5?	8 take away 6?
4 take away 3?	9 take away 8?
5 take away 6?	10 take away 5?

C Use counters if you need to.
Write numbers for ✶'s:

☆ 8−2=✶   6

1 7−4=✶	6 9−6=✶
2 8−1=✶	7 7−5=✶
3 6−4=✶	8 8−7=✶
4 9−5=✶	9 7−5=✶
5 8−7=✶	10 9−9=✶

penny
1p

two pence
2p

five pence
5p

A Name these coins:

☆ penny 1p

1

2

B How much money in each bag?

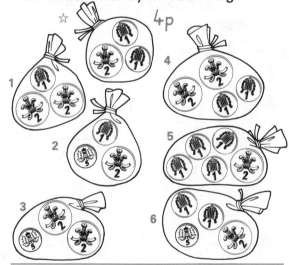

☆ 4p

1

2

3

4

5

6

C How much altogether?

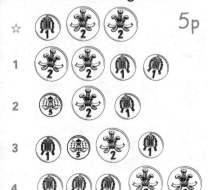

☆ 5p

1

2

3

4

D How much money?

☆ 2p+5p= ✳ 7p

1 2p+2p= ✳   6 4p+3p= ✳

2 1p+5p= ✳   7 2p+6p= ✳

3 5p+2p= ✳   8 5p+4p= ✳

4 5p+2p+1p= ✳   9 7p+1p= ✳

5 2p+1p+2p= ✳   10 5p+3p+1p= ✳

E 2p is taken from each box.
How much is left?

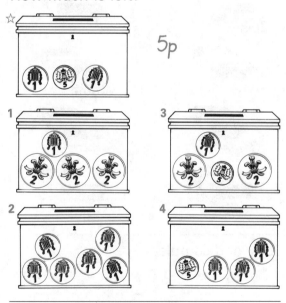

☆ 5p

1

2

3

4

F How much is left when:

☆ Mike has 9p and spends 4p? 5p

1 Mary has 8p and spends 3p?

2 Jo has 7p and spends 5p?

3 Paula has 6p and spends 2p?

4 Jim has 9p and spends 8p?

5 Ann has 7p and spends 7p?

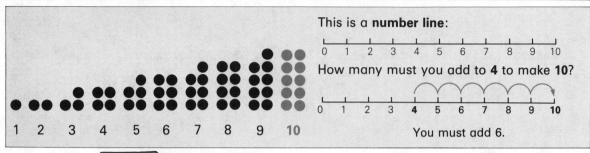

This is a **number line**:

How many must you add to **4** to make **10**?

You must add 6.

A 1 box holds 10 pencils.

How many more pencils to fill each box?

 2

 1

 2   5

 3   6

 4   7

         8

B Copy and complete:

☆ 3   *   *   6   *   *   9   10

   3   4   5   6   7   8   9   10

1   0   *   *   3   *   5   *

2   4   *   *   7   *   *   10

3   2   *   4   *   *   7   *

4   5   *   *   8   *   *

5   *   1   *   *   4   *   *

6   4   *   *   *   *   9   *

C How many must you add to these numbers to make 10?

☆ eight   2

1 nine   4 one   7 three

2 seven   5 six   8 nought

3 five   6 two

D Use coins if you need to.
There should be 10p in each box.
How much is missing?

☆  6p

1    5

2    6

3    7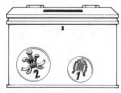

4    8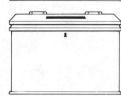

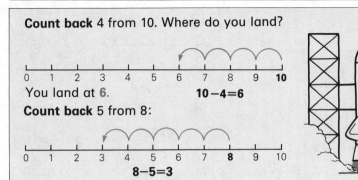

Count back 4 from 10. Where do you land?

You land at **6**.   **10−4=6**

Count back 5 from 8:

8−5=3

ten, nine, eight seven, six, five, four, three, two, one, zero . . .

A Where do you land when you **count back**:

☆ 5 from 9?

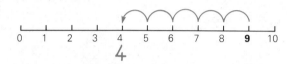
4

1 4 from 7?

2 3 from 8?

3 2 from 9?

4 3 from 7?

5 5 from 10?

6 4 from 9?

7 6 from 10?

8 4 from 10?

B Pencils come in boxes of ten.

How many left when:

☆ 3 are taken? 7

1 2 are taken?   6 0 are taken?

2 6 are taken?   7 8 are taken?

3 5 are taken?   8 10 are taken?

4 1 is taken?   9 7 are taken?

5 4 are taken?   10 9 are taken?

C Write numbers for ✱'s:

☆ 7−2=✱   5

1 6−3=✱   6 9−3=✱

2 5−1=✱   7 10−6=✱

3 7−4=✱   8 9−7=✱

4 8−3=✱   9 10−4=✱

5 8−5=✱   10 5−4=✱

D How many marbles are left if:

☆ Jo has 8 and loses 5? 3

1 Mary has 7 and loses 3?

2 Jim has 5 and loses 4?

3 Ann has 10 and loses 3?

4 Jill has 9 and loses 6?

5 Mike has 10 and loses 5?

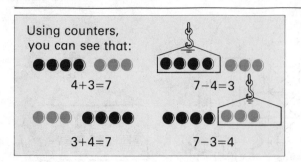

Using counters,
you can see that:

4+3=7

7−4=3

3+4=7

7−3=4

(number line 0 to 10)

7+1 > 2+4

means 7+1 is greater than 2+4
or   8   is greater than   6

A Use counters if you need to.
Write numbers for ✱'s:

☆

5+3=✱   8
3+5=✱   8
8−3=✱   5
8−✱ =3   5

1
4+2=✱
2+✱ =6
6−4=✱
6−✱ =4

5
7+✱ =9
✱ +7=9
9−2=✱
9−✱ =2

2
5+✱ =7
✱ +5=7
7−5=✱
7−2=✱

6
2+8=✱
8+✱ =10
10−✱ =2
10−✱ =8

3
6+✱ =9
✱ +6=9
9−✱ =3
9−✱ =6

7
3+4=✱
4+✱ =7
7−3=✱
✱ −4=3

4
3+✱ =5
✱ +3=5
5−✱ =2
5−2=✱

8
4+✱ =9
5+✱ =9
9−✱ =5
✱ −5=4

B Write the sign > < or = for ✱'s:

☆ 6+3✱2+5   >

1 2+6✱4+1   **9** 5+3✱3+5
2 9+0✱3+2   **10** 4+1✱1+5
3 4+3✱3+4   **11** 6+2✱7−3
4 7+1✱2+4   **12** 8+1✱8−1
5 2+7✱8+2   **13** 6+3✱3+6
6 4+4✱3+5   **14** 8−5✱8−3
7 7+2✱2+7   **15** 4−2✱4+2
8 6+4✱3+6   **16** 6+4✱4+6

C How many birds must be added to
each flock to make 10 altogether?

☆   3

1

2

3

D Write numbers for ✱'s:

☆ 8+✱ =10   2

1 6+✱ =10   **7** 4+✱ =10
2 4+6=✱   **8** 2+✱ =10
3 7+✱ =10   **9** 0+✱ =10
4 3+7=✱   **10** 1+✱ =10
5 9+✱ =10   **11** 5+✱ =10
6 1+9=✱   **12** 3+✱ =10

A Write these numbers in words:

1 6   6 7
2 8   7 1
3 10   8 3
4 5   9 9
5 2   10 0

B Write these numbers in order, **smallest first**:

1 6 9 1 10 5
2 4 7 1 9 2
3 10 6 0 5 4
4 3 2 8 9 1
5 0 9 5 3 10
6 5 2 7 10 6
7 3 8 0 5 1
8 10 6 3 7 0

C Write numbers for ✳'s:

1 $4+3=$ ✳   8 $2+6=$ ✳
2 $3+4=$ ✳   9 $5+5=$ ✳
3 $5+2=$ ✳   10 $9+0=$ ✳
4 $2+6=$ ✳   11 $1+8=$ ✳
5 $6+3=$ ✳   12 $0+10=$ ✳
6 $7+2=$ ✳   13 $3+5=$ ✳
7 $4+5=$ ✳   14 $6+4=$ ✳

D Write numbers for ✳'s:

1 $9-3=$ ✳   8 $9-6=$ ✳
2 $7-5=$ ✳   9 $5-2=$ ✳
3 $8-6=$ ✳   10 $8-5=$ ✳
4 $10-3=$ ✳   11 $9-5=$ ✳
5 $6-5=$ ✳   12 $7-2=$ ✳
6 $8-0=$ ✳   13 $8-3=$ ✳
7 $7-7=$ ✳   14 $6-0=$ ✳

E Write numbers for ✳'s:

1 $6+$ ✳ $=8$ 6 $3+$ ✳ $=10$
2 $2+$ ✳ $=4$ 7 $3+$ ✳ $=7$
3 $1+$ ✳ $=8$ 8 $6+$ ✳ $=10$
4 $4+$ ✳ $=10$ 9 $8+$ ✳ $=8$
5 $5+$ ✳ $=8$ 10 $1+$ ✳ $=10$

F How much money in each bag?

1

3

2

4

G You have 10 pence.
How much left when you spend:

1 4 pence?   6 3 pence?
2 2 pence?   7 5 pence?
3 7 pence?   8 8 pence?
4 9 pence?   9 6 pence?
5 1 penny?   10 10 pence?

H Write the sign < or > for ✳'s:

1 8 ✳ 6 6 7 ✳ $2+3$
2 3 ✳ 10 7 4 ✳ $3+5$
3 $3+2$ ✳ 7 8 $2+1$ ✳ $3+2$
4 $4+1$ ✳ 8 9 $4+5$ ✳ $6+2$
5 $6+3$ ✳ 8 10 $6+1$ ✳ $8+2$

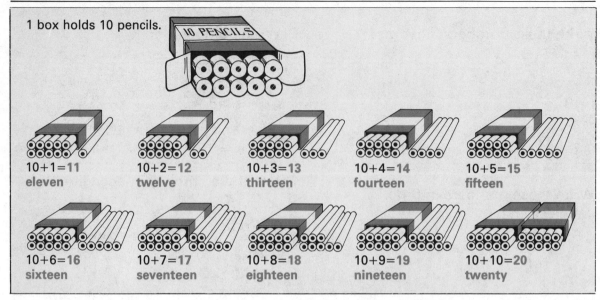

1 box holds 10 pencils.

10+1=11 eleven
10+2=12 twelve
10+3=13 thirteen
10+4=14 fourteen
10+5=15 fifteen

10+6=16 sixteen
10+7=17 seventeen
10+8=18 eighteen
10+9=19 nineteen
10+10=20 twenty

A Write in figures:

☆ thirteen   13

1 nineteen   6 twelve
2 eleven   7 twenty
3 fifteen   8 fourteen
4 eighteen   9 seventeen
5 sixteen   10 ten

B Write these numbers in words:

☆ 15   fifteen

1 13   5 14   8 17
2 19   6 18   9 11
3 12   7 10   10 20
4 16

C Write these numbers in tens and units:

☆ 11   1 ten 1 unit

1 12   6 19
2 13   7 17
3 14   8 18
4 15   9 10
5 16   10 20

D How many pencils in each group?

☆   16

1

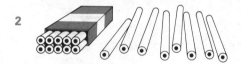

2

3

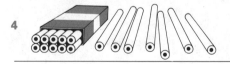

4

E Write the number that is:

☆ 1 ten and 4 units   14

1 1 ten and 2 units   6 1 ten and 9 units
2 1 ten and 5 units   7 1 ten and 6 units
3 1 ten and 7 units   8 1 ten and 8 units
4 1 ten and 3 units   9 1 ten and 1 unit
5 1 ten and 0 units   10 2 tens and 0 units

Numbers to 20

0 1 2 3 4 5 6 7 8 9 10 11 12 13 14 15 16 17 18 19 20

A What number comes **between**:

☆ eleven and thirteen? 12

1 twelve and fourteen?

2 sixteen and eighteen?

3 ten and twelve?

4 seventeen and nineteen?

5 nine and eleven?

6 thirteen and fifteen?

7 nought and two?

8 eighteen and twenty?

B Write these numbers in order, **smallest first**:

☆ 12 14 7 9 11

  7 9 11 12 14

1 13 8 5 11 10

2 16 17 20 19 15

3 8 12 10 9 11

4 16 14 11 9 15

5 6 15 0 20 12

6 18 2 14 9 20

C Write in words:

☆ 1 ten 6 units sixteen

1 1 ten 4 units   6 1 ten 7 units

2 1 ten 1 unit   7 1 ten 2 units

3 1 ten 5 units   8 1 ten 8 units

4 1 ten 9 units   9 1 ten 0 units

5 1 ten 3 units   10 2 tens 0 units

D Write these numbers in tens and units:

☆ 18 1 ten and 8 units

1 15   6 20

2 17   7 16

3 11   8 12

4 19   9 10

5 14   10 13

E Use counters if you need to. Write numbers for ✻'s:

☆ 10+6= ✻ 16

1 10+5= ✻   6 10+8= ✻

2 10+1= ✻   7 10+2= ✻

3 10+9= ✻   8 10+7= ✻

4 10+0= ✻   9 10+4= ✻

5 10+3= ✻   10 10+10= ✻

F Write these numbers in order, **largest first**:

☆ 16 12 14 19 8

  19 16 14 12 8

1 15 17 9 11 10

2 18 15 20 17 19

3 14 8 10 12 13

4 15 11 9 10 8

5 0 6 11 9 12

6 14 20 4 10 0

7 3 12 19 8 14

8 17 5 16 9 11

9 6 14 18 7 13

10 3 15 8 12 1

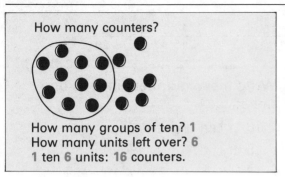

How many counters?

How many groups of ten? **1**
How many units left over? **6**
1 ten **6** units: **16** counters.

A Write how many counters in 2
   different ways:

☆    I ten and 3 units   13

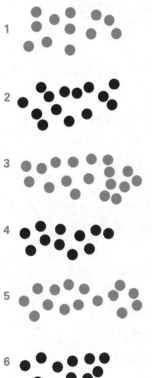

1

2

3

4

5

6

7

8

B Copy and complete this table:

		10	I ten and O units	10+0
☆	ten	10	I ten and O units	10+0
1	eleven			
2	twelve			
3	thirteen			
4	fourteen			
5	fifteen			
6	sixteen			
7	seventeen			
8	eighteen			
9	nineteen			
10	twenty			

C How many units altogether?

☆ 1 ten and 4 units   14 units

1 1 ten and 6 units   6 1 ten and 7 units

2 1 ten and 3 units   7 1 ten and 2 units

3 1 ten and 0 units   8 1 ten and 8 units

4 1 ten and 9 units   9 1 ten and 1 unit

5 1 ten and 5 units   10 2 tens and 0 units

D Sweets are put into packs of 10.
   How many left over with:

☆ 12 sweets?   2

1 16 sweets?   6 10 sweets?

2 11 sweets?   7 13 sweets?

3 17 sweets?   8 20 sweets?

4 14 sweets?   9 15 sweets?

5 19 sweets?   10 18 sweets?

Numbers to 20

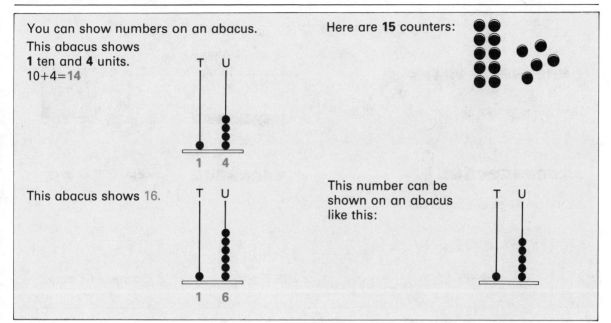

You can show numbers on an abacus.
This abacus shows
1 ten and **4** units.
10+4=**14**

1   4

This abacus shows 16.

1   6

Here are **15** counters:

This number can be
shown on an abacus
like this:

A Write the number shown on each abacus:

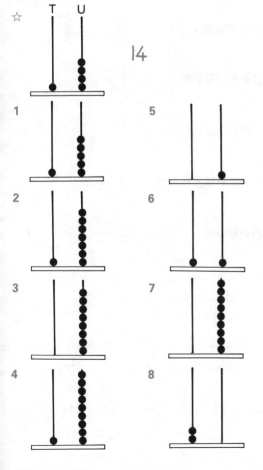

☆   14

1

5

2

6

3

7

4

8

B Draw an abacus picture to show how many counters in each group:

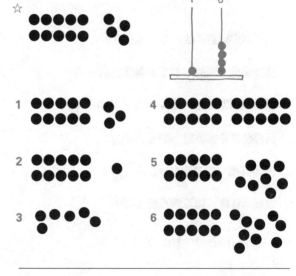

☆

1   4

2   5

3   6

C Draw abacus pictures to show these numbers:

☆ 13

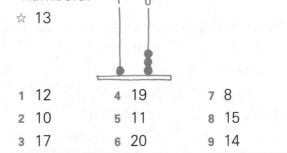

1 12	4 19	7 8
2 10	5 11	8 15
3 17	6 20	9 14

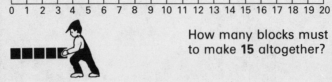

How many blocks altogether? 7+5= *

There are **12** blocks altogether.

7+5=**12**

How many blocks must be added to make **15** altogether?

8 + * =15

7

8+ 7 =15   **7** blocks must be added.

A Write how many altogether:

 13

1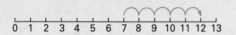

2

3

4

5

6

B Write numbers for * 's:

☆ 7+5= *   12

1 6+4= *   9 6+7= *

2 4+6= *   10 7+6= *

3 9+6= *   11 8+8= *

4 6+9= *   12 9+9= *

5 11+5= *   13 5+5= *

6 5+11= *   14 7+7= *

7 8+9= *   15 6+6= *

8 9+8= *   16 10+10= *

C How many blocks must be added to these piles to make 16 altogether?

☆  7

1

2

3

4

D Use a number line if you need to. Write numbers for * 's:

☆ 12+ * =17   5

1 6+ * =10   7 7+ * =14

2 4+ * =10   8 9+ * =18

3 8+ * =11   9 6+ * =12

4 3+ * =11   10 15+ * =16

5 7+ * =13   11 13+ * =19

6 6+ * =13   12 14+ * =20

Numbers to 20

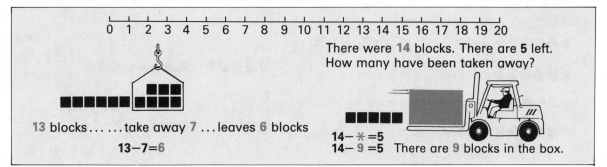

0 1 2 3 4 5 6 7 8 9 10 11 12 13 14 15 16 17 18 19 20

13 blocks......take away 7 ...leaves 6 blocks

13−7=6

There were **14** blocks. There are **5** left.
How many have been taken away?

14− ✳ =5
14− 9 =5   There are **9** blocks in the box.

A Write how many are left:

☆ 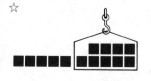 $14-9=5$

1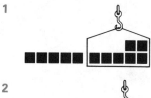

2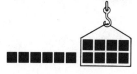

3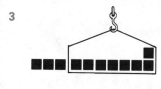

4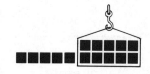

C There were 13 blocks.
How many have been taken away?

☆  10

1

2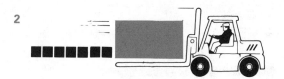

3

B Use a number line if you need to.
Write numbers for ✳'s:

☆ 12−6= ✳ 6

1 10−7= ✳	7 17−4= ✳
2 10−4= ✳	8 19−10= ✳
3 11−6= ✳	9 14−10= ✳
4 14−5= ✳	10 19−12= ✳
5 15−7= ✳	11 20−14= ✳
6 18−6= ✳	12 20−16= ✳

D Use a number line if you need to.
Write numbers for ✳'s:

☆ 16−✳=7 9

1 12−✳=8	7 19−✳=10
2 12−✳=4	8 20−✳=14
3 15−✳=6	9 16−✳=8
4 15−✳=9	10 13−✳=6
5 17−✳=6	11 14−✳=8
6 17−✳=11	12 20−✳=11

Using counters you can see that:

9+6=15

6+9=15

15−9=6

15−6=9

If you know that 8+6=14,
you can write 3 more facts:
6+8=14   14−6=8   14−8=6

A Use counters if you need to.
Write numbers for ✳'s:

☆
8+5=✳ 13   13−8=✳ 5
5+8=✳ 13   13−✳=8 5

1
6+7=✳   13−6=✳
7+✳=13   13−✳=6

2
5+6=✳   11−✳=6
✳+5=11   11−✳=5

3
7+✳=15   15−✳=8
8+✳=15   15−✳=7

4
9+5=✳   14−✳=5
5+✳=14   14−✳=9

5
7+✳=16   16−✳=9
✳+7=16   16−9=✳

6
8+9=✳   17−✳=9
9+✳=17   17−9=✳

B Write 3 more facts for each of these:

☆
7+5=12   5+7=12
             12−7=5
             12−5=7

1
7+4=11

2
8+3=11

3
5+7=12

4
9+4=13

5
7+8=15

6
6+9=15

C How many socks must be added to
each line to make 18 altogether?

**ten pence
10p**

A How much money in each box?

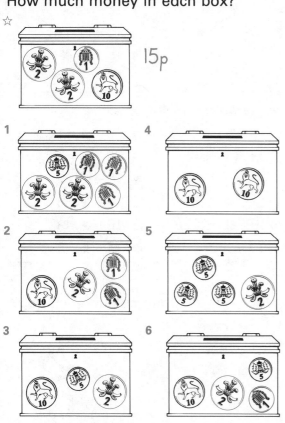

☆ 15p

B How much money?

☆ 4p+7p= ✳ 11p

1 3p+6p= ✳   7 8p+9p= ✳
2 5p+5p= ✳   8 10p+5p= ✳
3 4p+8p= ✳   9 11p+6p= ✳
4 9p+5p= ✳   10 9p+11p= ✳
5 6p+8p= ✳   11 12p+7p= ✳
6 9p+7p= ✳   12 10p+10p= ✳

C What is the hidden coin in each bag?

☆ 10p 2p

D Use coins if you need to.
How much left if:

☆ Ben has 12p and spends 5p?   7p
1 Paula has 10p and spends 3p?
2 Ann has 14p and spends 8p?
3 Jill has 18p and spends 10p?
4 Carl has 16p and spends 11p?
5 Kim has 19p and spends 14p?

E How much money?

☆ 15p−8p= ✳   7p

1 10p−6p= ✳   6 20p−7p= ✳
2 10p−4p= ✳   7 20p−12p= ✳
3 12p−7p= ✳   8 13p−9p= ✳
4 13p−8p= ✳   9 15p−7p= ✳
5 14p−6p= ✳   10 16p−8p= ✳

A Write **in words** the number that is:

1 1 ten and 4 units   6 1 ten and 0 units

2 1 ten and 6 units   7 1 ten and 5 units

3 1 ten and 3 units   8 1 ten and 8 units

4 1 ten and 1 unit   9 2 tens and 0 units

5 1 ten and 7 units   10 1 ten and 9 units

B Write these numbers in order, smallest first:

1 16   7   12   10   4

2 19   14   2   17   10

3 11   12   15   1   8

4 16   6   5   14   20

5 13   2   15   4   17

C How many counters in these groups?

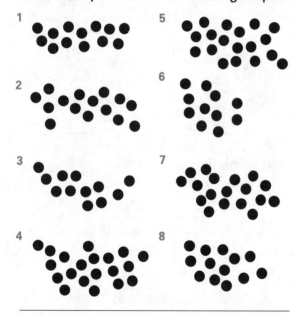

D Pencils are put into packs of 10. How many left over with:

1 16 pencils?   6 19 pencils?

2 12 pencils?   7 15 pencils?

3 11 pencils?   8 20 pencils?

4 18 pencils?   9 17 pencils?

5 10 pencils?   10 14 pencils?

E Write numbers for ✳'s:

1 $10+7=$✳   6 $14+5=$✳

2 $13+5=$✳   7 $8+7=$✳

3 $8+6=$✳   8 $9+9=$✳

4 $7+9=$✳   9 $4+10=$✳

5 $8+11=$✳   10 $16+3=$✳

F Write numbers for ✳'s:

1 $16-7=$✳   6 $17-10=$✳

2 $14-9=$✳   7 $18-8=$✳

3 $20-10=$✳   8 $19-11=$✳

4 $12-4=$✳   9 $15-7=$✳

5 $13-8=$✳   10 $16-14=$✳

G Write numbers for ✳'s:

1 $14+$✳$=16$ 7 $15-$✳$=12$

2 $9+$✳$=15$ 8 $20-$✳$=10$

3 $4+$✳$=12$ 9 $18-$✳$=9$

4 $11+$✳$=18$ 10 $14-$✳$=8$

5 $10+$✳$=20$ 11 $16-$✳$=9$

6 $8+$✳$=8$ 12 $14-$✳$=3$

H What is the hidden coin in each bag?

Numbers to 100

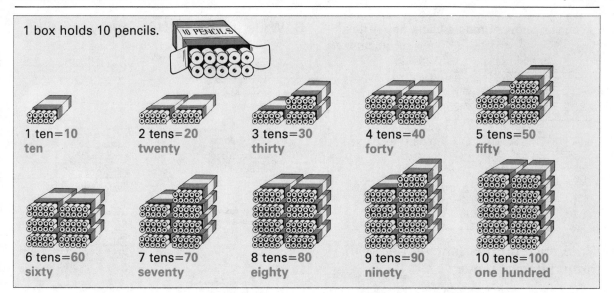

1 box holds 10 pencils. 10 PENCILS

| 1 ten=10 ten | 2 tens=20 twenty | 3 tens=30 thirty | 4 tens=40 forty | 5 tens=50 fifty |
| 6 tens=60 sixty | 7 tens=70 seventy | 8 tens=80 eighty | 9 tens=90 ninety | 10 tens=100 one hundred |

A Write in figures:

☆ fifty   50

1 thirty   6 ninety

2 seventy   7 eighty

3 one hundred   8 sixty

4 ten   9 twenty

5 forty

B Write these numbers as words:

☆ 60   sixty

1 90   6 100

2 10   7 70

3 40   8 80

4 30   9 50

5 20

C How many units in:

☆ 3 tens?   thirty

1 5 tens?   6 2 tens?

2 9 tens?   7 4 tens?

3 1 ten?   8 6 tens?

4 8 tens?   9 10 tens?

5 7 tens?

D How many tens in:

☆ 40? 4

1 60?   6 50?

2 30?   7 100?

3 80?   8 70?

4 10?   9 20?

5 90?

E Write these numbers as words:

☆ 6 tens 0 units   sixty

1 4 tens 0 units   6 5 tens 0 units

2 7 tens 0 units   7 10 tens 0 units

3 9 tens 0 units   8 2 tens 0 units

4 3 tens 0 units   9 1 ten 0 units

5 8 tens 0 units

F Write these numbers in tens and units:

☆ 20   2 tens 0 units

1 30   6 40

2 70   7 100

3 50   8 80

4 60   9 10

5 90

You can show numbers using **apparatus**:

3 tens and 5 units
30+5=35
thirty-five

5 tens and 7 units
50+7=57
fifty-seven

A Write each number shown below in three different ways:

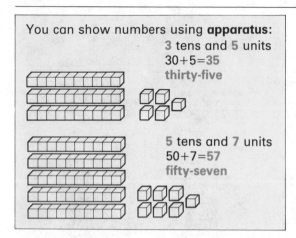

☆ 2 tens and
6 units
26
twenty-six

1

2

3

4

5

6

B Write in **words**. How many pencils?

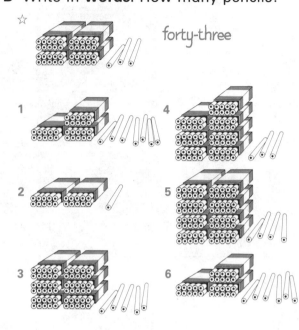

☆ forty-three

1

4

2

5

3

6

C Write in **figures**. How many sweets?

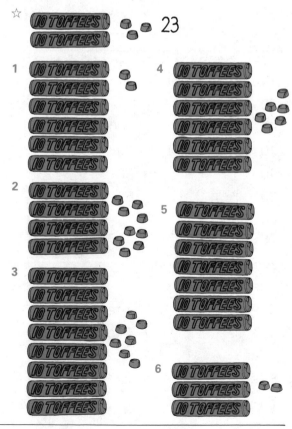

☆ 23

1 4

2 5

3 6

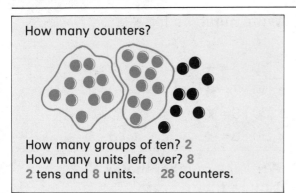

How many counters?

How many groups of ten? **2**
How many units left over? **8**
2 tens and **8** units.   **28** counters.

A Write how many counters in 2 different ways:

☆

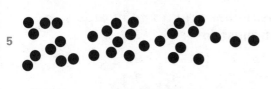

3 tens and 6 units   36

1

2

3

4

5

6

7

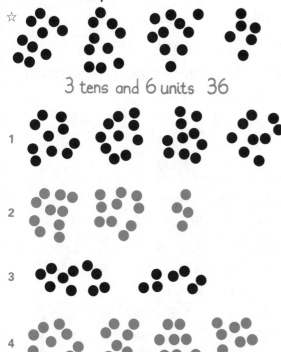

B Use counters if you need to. How many groups of ten counters can you make with:

☆ 34 counters?   3

1 23 counters?   6 92 counters?
2 47 counters?   7 79 counters?
3 61 counters?   8 54 counters?
4 59 counters?   9 85 counters?
5 30 counters?   10 100 counters?

C Sweets are put in packs of 10.

How many left over with:

☆ 46 sweets?   6

1 21 sweets?   6 35 sweets?
2 54 sweets?   7 80 sweets?
3 17 sweets?   8 95 sweets?
4 36 sweets?   9 50 sweets?
5 62 sweets?   10 99 sweets?

D Write in figures:

☆ twenty-nine   29

1 twenty-six   6 ninety-four
2 fifty-one   7 eighty-seven
3 sixty-eight   8 thirty
4. forty-nine   9 sixty-four
5 seventeen   10 fifty-three

E Write these numbers as words:

☆ 37   thirty-seven

1 49   6 21   11 12
2 76   7 53   12 48
3 35   8 78   13 81
4 92   9 96   14 67
5 17   10 38   15 99

	UNITS									
	0	1	2	3	4	5	6	7	8	9
0	0	1	2	3	4	5	6	7	8	9
1	10	11	12	13	14	15	16	17	18	19
2	20	21	22	23	24	25	26	27	28	29
3	30	31	32	33	34	35	36	37	38	39
T E N S 4	40	41	42	43	44	45	46	47	48	49
5	50	51	52	53	54	55	56	57	58	59
6	60	61	62	63	64	65	66	67	68	69
7	70	71	72	73	74	75	76	77	78	79
8	80	81	82	83	84	85	86	87	88	89
9	90	91	92	93	94	95	96	97	98	99
10	100									

A Write these numbers in **tens** and **units**:

☆ 46   4 tens 6 units

1 38   5 92   9 53
2 19   6 27   10 88
3 57   7 72   11 64
4 43   8 35   12 41

B Write the number that is:

☆ 6 tens and 3 units   63

1 3 tens and 2 units
2 9 tens and 7 units
3 2 tens and 0 units
4 7 tens and 7 units
5 0 tens and 5 units
6 6 tens and 8 units
7 8 tens and 6 units
8 5 tens and 1 unit
9 1 ten and 5 units
10 10 tens and 0 units
11 3 tens and 6 units
12 8 tens and 2 units

C Write numbers for ✳'s:

☆ 70+6=✳ 76

1 20+3=✳   5 30+4=✳
2 40+7=✳   6 70+6=✳
3 90+9=✳   7 50+0=✳
4 20+8=✳   8 40+5=✳

D Write the number that is **1 more than**:

☆ 37   38

1 24   4 90   7 19
2 65   5 69   8 88
3 19   6 10   9 59

E Write the number that is **1 less than**:

☆ 32   31

1 57   4 61   7 11
2 79   5 34   8 20
3 92   6 68   9 80

F Copy and complete:

☆ 26 ✳ 28 ✳ 30 ✳ ✳

26 27 28 29 30 31 32

1 43 ✳ ✳ 46 ✳ ✳ ✳ 50
2 28 ✳ ✳ ✳ 32 ✳ 34 ✳
3 79 ✳ ✳ 82 ✳ ✳ ✳ 86
4 93 ✳ 95 ✳ ✳ 98 ✳ ✳
5 ✳ 17 ✳ ✳ ✳ ✳ 22 ✳

G Write these numbers in order, **smallest first**:

☆ 43 26 84 52 90

26 43 52 84 90

1 35 79 14 50 22
2 96 75 92 70 87
3 63 36 60 30 66
4 19 91 22 99 11
5 10 100 1 11 0

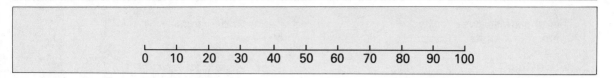

0 10 20 30 40 50 60 70 80 90 100

A Write numbers for ✱'s:

☆ 10 ✱ ✱ 40 ✱ ✱ 70

10 20 30 40 50 60 70

1 30 ✱ ✱ ✱ 70 ✱ 90
2 0 ✱ ✱ 30 ✱ ✱ 60
3 20 ✱ ✱ 50 ✱ 70 ✱
4 40 ✱ ✱ ✱ 80 90 ✱

B Write the number that is **10 less than**:

☆ seventy *sixty*

1 thirty   5 twenty
2 sixty   6 ninety
3 forty   7 fifty
4 eighty   8 one hundred

C **Count in tens.**
Copy and complete:

☆ 3 ✱ ✱ 33 ✱ ✱ 63

3 13 23 33 43 53 63

1 5 ✱ ✱ ✱ 45 ✱ 65
2 22 ✱ ✱ 52 ✱ ✱ 82
3 37 ✱ 57 ✱ ✱ 87 ✱
4 19 ✱ ✱ ✱ ✱ 69 79

D **Count back in tens.**
Copy and complete:

☆ 72 ✱ ✱ 42 ✱ ✱ 12

72 62 52 42 32 22 12

1 85 ✱ ✱ ✱ 45 ✱ 25
2 71 ✱ 51 ✱ ✱ 21 ✱
3 98 ✱ ✱ 68 ✱ ✱ 38
4 77 ✱ ✱ 47 ✱ ✱ 17

E How many **ten pence** are worth:

☆ 50p? 5

1 40p?   4 80p?   7 10p?
2 70p?   5 60p?   8 20p?
3 30p?   6 90p?

F How many tens?

☆ 4 tens+3 tens   ☆ 5 tens−2 tens

7 tens   3 tens

1 6 tens+3 tens   6 8 tens−4 tens
2 4 tens+2 tens   7 9 tens−5 tens
3 5 tens+4 tens   8 10 tens−5 tens
4 3 tens+5 tens   9 7 tens−5 tens
5 3 tens+3 tens   10 9 tens−8 tens

G Write numbers for ✱'s:

☆ 40+20= ✱ 60

1 30+10=✱   6 40+40=✱
2 40+30=✱   7 30+40=✱
3 60+20=✱   8 20+70=✱
4 50+40=✱   9 30+50=✱
5 70+20=✱   10 50+50=✱

H How much money altogether if:

☆ John has 50p and
is given 20p?   70p

1 Sharon is given 40p and then 30p more?
2 Anne is given 60p then another 30p?
3 Mike has 70p and is given 20p more?
4 Alan has 40p and is given 50p more?
5 Joy is given 30p and then another 40p?
6 Trevor has 50p and is given 20p more?
7 Dennis is given 20p then 60p more?

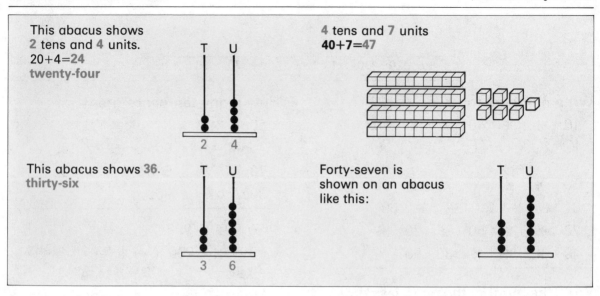

This abacus shows
2 tens and 4 units.
20+4=24
twenty-four

This abacus shows 36.
thirty-six

4 tens and 7 units
40+7=47

Forty-seven is
shown on an abacus
like this:

A Write these abacus numbers in
2 different ways:

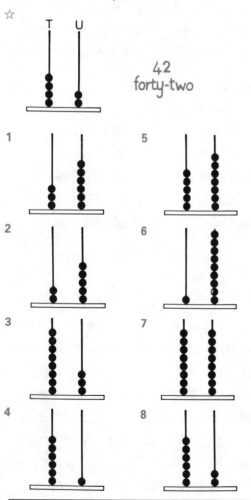

42
forty-two

B Draw an abacus picture to show
how many in each group:

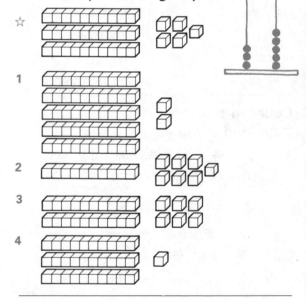

C Draw abacus pictures to show
these numbers:

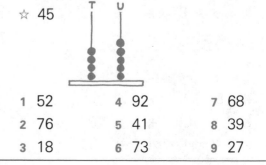

☆ 45

1	52	4	92	7	68
2	76	5	41	8	39
3	18	6	73	9	27

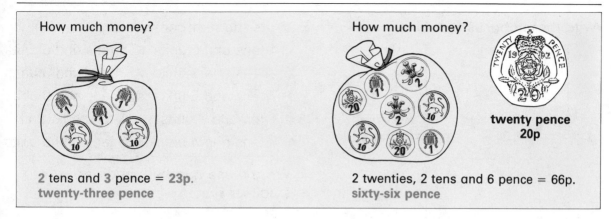

How much money?

2 tens and **3** pence = **23p**.
twenty-three pence

How much money?

twenty pence
20p

2 twenties, 2 tens and 6 pence = 66p.
sixty-six pence

A Write how much money in 3 different ways:

B Write how much money in 2 different ways:

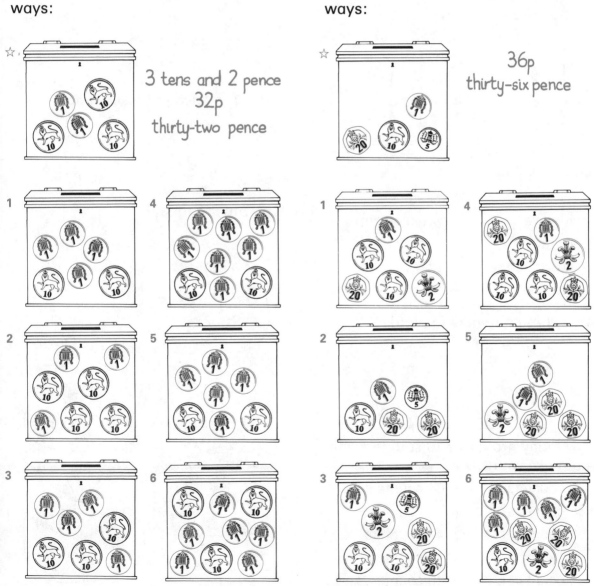

☆ 3 tens and 2 pence
32p
thirty-two pence

☆ 36p
thirty-six pence

1

2

3

4

5

6

1

2

3

4

5

6

A Write these abacus numbers:

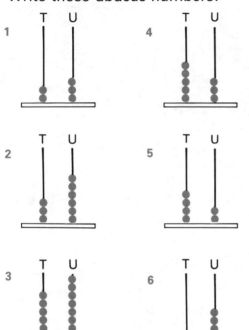

B Write in figures:

1 fifty-one
2 thirty-five
3 seventy-six
4 ninety-three
5 sixty-nine
6 eleven
7 twenty-eight
8 forty-two
9 eighty-seven
10 seventeen

C Write these numbers in words:

1 37
2 29
3 69
4 88
5 19
6 70
7 43
8 93
9 46
10 50
11 24
12 16

D How many groups of 10 counters can you make with:

1 27 counters?
2 35 counters?
3 51 counters?
4 93 counters?
5 89 counters?
6 64 counters?
7 72 counters?
8 47 counters?
9 16 counters?
10 26 counters?

E Write the number that is:

1 4 tens and 5 units
2 2 tens and 8 units
3 7 tens and 6 units
4 1 ten and 9 units
5 8 tens and 4 units
6 5 tens and 6 units
7 9 tens and 3 units
8 3 tens and 9 units
9 1 ten and 1 unit
10 6 tens and 5 units

F Write these numbers in order, **smallest first**:

1 26 17 39 41 60
2 92 71 17 63 35
3 30 16 13 62 90
4 27 72 36 63 13
5 87 88 78 77 79

G Add 10 to each of these numbers:

1 26
2 19
3 42
4 64
5 53
6 47
7 82
8 60
9 36
10 28
11 49
12 62

H How much money?

The Fishing game

16+4=
12+5=
5+9=
15−9=
8+7=
19−7=
10−4=
11+8=
60+20=
15−7=

Bob
Fred
Jane
Ann
Mike
Trevor
Ben
Alex
Beverley
Steve

12
18
19
6
30
16
8
70
8
15

Five people have
caught the right fish.
Write down their names.

A You need: 6 counters;
an abacus card;
a copy of a number grid (see teacher's book)

Tens	Units
	●
	●

When you put 2 counters on an abacus card you can make the numbers 2, 11 or 20. (See picture)

On your number grid, colour in yellow the squares showing the numbers 2, 11 and 20.

Tens	Units
●	
	●

Using your abacus card, work out the numbers you can make with 3 counters.

Colour these numbers in green on your number grid.

Colour in red the numbers you can make with 4 counters.

Colour in blue the numbers you can make with 5 counters.

Tens	Units
●	
●	

Colour in brown the numbers you can make with 6 counters.

Your number grid will help you to answer the next question.

Write the numbers you can make on an abacus card with:
1) 7 counters   2) 8 counters   3) 9 counters

B Write down 4 different sets of coins that can be used to make 5p.

How many different sets of coins can you find to make these amounts?

6p   8p   10p

Design your own money system using 4 different coins so that you can pay any amount up to £1.

What do you like about your money system?

C Long ago, people used different number systems.

Find out how these systems were used. Do you think our system is better? Explain your answer.

Spiders have 8 legs.
Invent a number system that would help spiders to count using their legs.

		1	2	3	4	5	6	7	8	9	10
Egyptian		I	II	III	IIII	III II	III III	IIII III	IIII III	III III III	∩
Roman		I	II	III	IV	V	VI	VII	VIII	IX	X
Mayan		●	●●	●●●	●●●●	▬	● ▬	●● ▬	●●● ▬	●●●● ▬	▬▬

Answer any questions you can. Leave those you cannot do.

1 Write the number that is one more than 7.

2 Write the number that is three less than 9.

3 Write the number that is four more than 8.

4 4 + 5 = ✳

5 7 + 0 = ✳

6 6 + 3 + 5 = ✳

7 8 − 5 = ✳

8 12 − 7 = ✳

9 How much is left when Jenny has 10p and spends 4p?

10 How much is left when Vikram has 20p and spends 12p?

11 How much is left when Sonia has 50p and spends 15p?

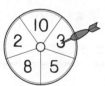

12 In this game what is the highest score you can make with three darts?

13 With three darts can you score 27?

14 Write in figures thirteen.

15 Write in figures thirty-seven.

16 Write in figures one hundred and six.

17 Write in words 19.

18 Write in words 18.

19 Write in words 112.

20 Write in words the number that is one ten and eight units.

21 Write these numbers in order with the largest first ... 26; 38; 19; 27; 30.

22 How many full packs of ten pencils can you make with 52 pencils?

23 How many full packs of ten candles can you make with 89 candles?

24 8 + 10 = ✳

25 14 + ✳ = 21

26 95 + ✳ = 102

27 13 − ✳ = 7

28 20 − ✳ = 14

29 45 − 7 = ✳

30 52 − 16 = ✳

31

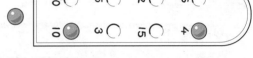

What must be scored with the third ball to make a total of 20?

32 How many units in 6 tens?

33 How many tens in 90?

34 Write the number that is 4 tens and 7 units.

For each abacus below write down the number that is shown.

35

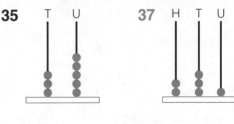

37

36

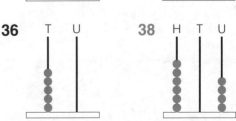

38

39 How much is left if you have £1 and spend 25p?

A Which is the **shorter** fish, red or black?

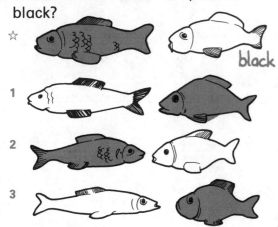

B Which is the **longer** rod, black or red?

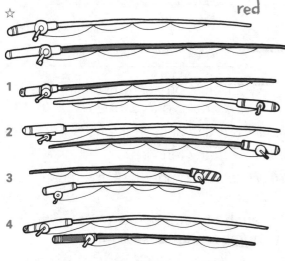

C Who is the **taller**?

D Which is the **narrower** glass, red or black?

E Which is the **thinner** string, red or black?

F 1 Is your pencil **longer** than this line?

2 Is your thumb **wider** than this thumb?

3 Are you **shorter** than your teacher?

4 Is your pencil **narrower** than your thumb?

Length

Distances can be measured in **metres**.

A **metre rule** can be used for measuring distances:

This door handle is about 1 metre from the floor.

The length of the bookcase is **greater than** 1 metre.

A Are these measures greater than 1 metre or less than 1 metre?

☆ the **length** of an aeroplane

greater

1 the **height** of your school

2 the **length** of a pin

3 the **height** of an elephant

4 the **length** of a key

5 the **length** of your arm

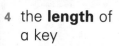

6 the **height** of your teacher

B Use a metre rule to answer these:

1 Is your classroom **more than** 8 metres long?

2 Is your desk **less than** 4 metres from the classroom door?

3 Are you **more than** 1 metre tall?

4 Is the classroom door **less than** 1 metre wide?

5 Is your teacher's desk **more than** 4 metres from your desk?

C Name 3 objects in your classroom that are:

1 **longer than** 1 metre

2 **shorter than** 1 metre

3 **about the same length as** 1 metre

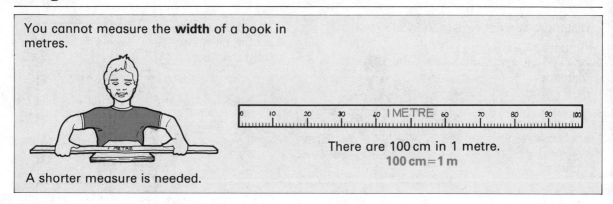

You cannot measure the **width** of a book in metres.

A shorter measure is needed.

There are 100 cm in 1 metre.
100 cm = 1 m

A Use a ruler to measure.
Write the lengths of these objects
in centimetres:

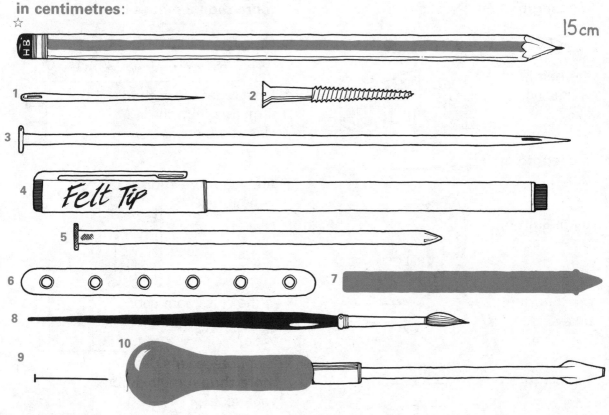

☆ 15 cm

1

2

3

4

5

6

7

8

9

10

B Write the lengths of these lines
in centimetres:

☆ —————————— 6 cm

1 ———

2 ——————————

3 —————————

4 ——————————

5 ——————————

C Draw **straight lines** of these lengths:

☆ 5 cm ——————————

1 7 cm   6 11 cm

2 9 cm   7 14 cm

3 2 cm   8 6 cm

4 12 cm   9 10 cm

5 15 cm   10 8 cm

Length

The Great Snail Escape!

The Snailery

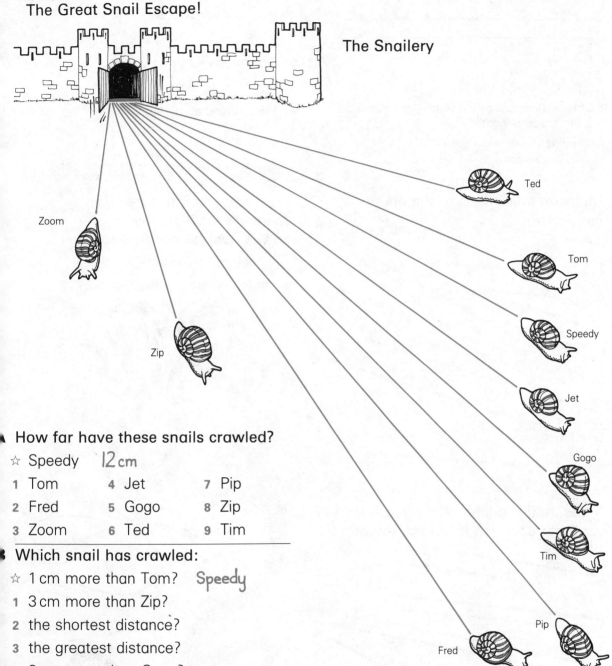

A How far have these snails crawled?

☆ Speedy   12 cm

1	Tom	4	Jet	7	Pip
2	Fred	5	Gogo	8	Zip
3	Zoom	6	Ted	9	Tim

B Which snail has crawled:

☆ 1 cm more than Tom?   Speedy

1 3 cm more than Zip?

2 the shortest distance?

3 the greatest distance?

4 3 cm more than Gogo?

5 5 cm less than Tim?

6 6 cm less than Fred?

7 5 cm more than Jet?

8 less than 4 cm?

9 further than Fred?

10 3 cm further than Zoom?

C Which snails have crawled:

☆ less than 10 cm?   Ted, Zip, Zoom

1 more than 5 cm?

2 between 5 cm and 10 cm?

3 further than Ted?

4 less than 14 cm?

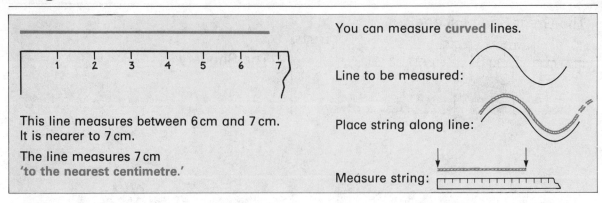

This line measures between 6 cm and 7 cm.
It is nearer to 7 cm.

The line measures 7 cm
'to the nearest centimetre.'

You can measure **curved** lines.

Line to be measured:

Place string along line:

Measure string:

A Measure these lines to the nearest centimetre:

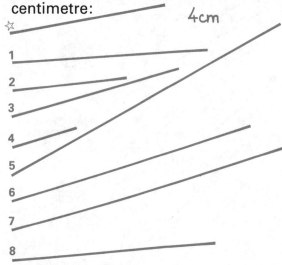

4 cm

☆

1

2

3

4

5

6

7

8

B Measure these lines to the nearest centimetre. Which is **longer**, red or black?

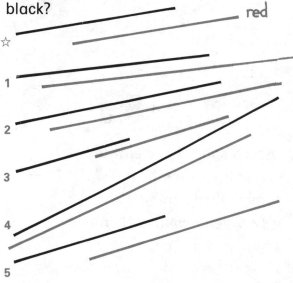

red

☆

1

2

3

4

5

C Use string to measure. Measure each snake **to the nearest centimetre**:

1 Which is the longest snake?

2 Which is the shortest snake?

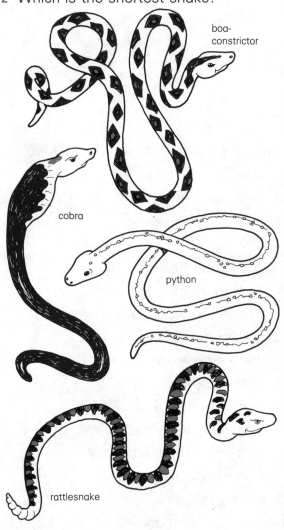

boa-constrictor

cobra

python

rattlesnake

A This length is your **reach**. Is your reach longer or shorter than your height?

Is this the same for the other children in your class?

Is the person with the longest reach also the tallest person in the class?

A man went into a shop to order a hat. When he was asked what size, he said that the distance around his head was about the same as the length of his arm from his shoulder to his wrist. Could that have been true?

Would this be a good way for you to find a hat of the right size?

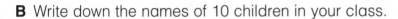

B Write down the names of 10 children in your class.

Without asking the children to stand up, try to write down their names in order of their heights with the shortest child first and the tallest one last.

Because the other children are likely to be busy, you must work out how to measure their heights one at a time. **You cannot stand two people side by side**.

Measure the heights of the ten children.

Write a new list with the children's names in order of height.

How many children were written in the right place on your first list?

C You need a partner for this activity.

Collect 5 different balls such as a tennis ball, a rubber ball, a 'super' ball, a table tennis ball and a golf ball.

Drop the first ball from a height of $1\frac{1}{2}$ metres near a wall.
Ask your partner to mark the top of the bounce.
Now drop the ball again to check your mark.

Repeat this for each of the balls.

Measure the height of each bounce to the nearest centimetre.

Which ball has the highest bounce?

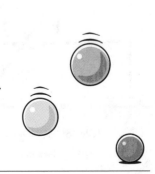

Do you find the same result if you drop each ball from a height of half a metre?

Answer any questions you can. Leave those you cannot do.

1 Who is the taller, Jamie or Selma?

2 Which is the longer shoe, red or black?

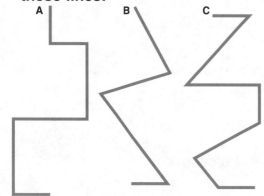

3 Is the length of your teacher's table longer or shorter than one metre?

4 Are you taller than one metre?

5 Is your classroom wider than 3 metres?

6 Is the height of your classroom door less than 2 metres?

Arun has measured:

> the length of his pencil,
>
> the width of a coin,
>
> the height of a bottle,
>
> the length of his table.

7 Which measure is 2 cm?

8 Which measure is $1\frac{1}{2}$ m?

9 Which measure is 32 cm?

10 Measure the length of each of these lines:

A   B   C

11 Which is the longest line?

12 Which is the shortest line?

Work out the lengths of these lines to the nearest centimetre.

13

14

15

Work out to the nearest centimetre:

16 the length of a page in this book.

17 the width of a page in this book.

Two pipes are joined end to end.

What is the total length when:

18 Pipe 1 is 8 m and Pipe 2 is 4 m?

19 Pipe 1 is 9 m and Pipe 2 is 11 m?

20 Pipe 1 is 20 m and pipe 2 is 16 m?

21 A piece of string measures 19 m. How much remains when 11 m is cut off?

22 A lorry and trailer together measure 46 m. The trailer measures 15 m. How long is the lorry?

23 A plumber wants a pipeline that is 28 m long. Which three pieces of pipe should he join?

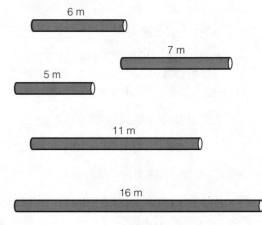

6 m

7 m

5 m

11 m

16 m

Weight

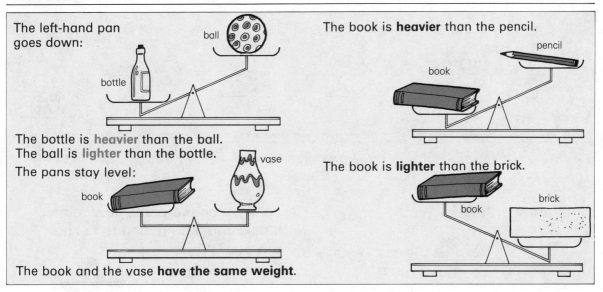

The left-hand pan goes down:

bottle / ball

The bottle is **heavier** than the ball.
The ball is **lighter** than the bottle.

The pans stay level:

book / vase

The book and the vase **have the same weight**.

The book is **heavier** than the pencil.

pencil / book

The book is **lighter** than the brick.

book / brick

A Which object is **lighter**?

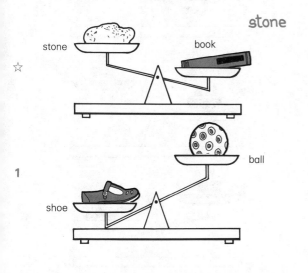

stone / book — stone

☆

1 ball / shoe

2 pencil / rubber

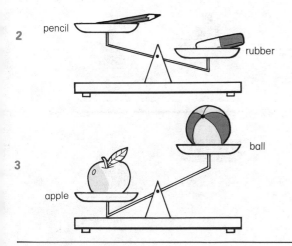

3 ball / apple

B Name 5 things in the classroom that you think are **heavier** than this book.

☆ blackboard

C Name 5 things in the classroom that you think are **lighter** than this book.

☆ crayon

D 1 Name 3 objects that you think are **about the same weight as** this book.

2 Use scales or a balance. Put the book on one pan. Put the objects one at a time on the other pan.

3 Copy and complete this table:

name of object	heavier or lighter than book

E Name 3 things that are lighter than your pencil.

☆ fly

F Name 3 things that are heavier than an elephant.

☆ jumbo jet

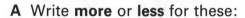

The cup weighs **more than** 4 blocks.

The cup weighs **the same as** 5 blocks.

The cup weighs **less than** 6 blocks.

A Write **more** or **less** for these:

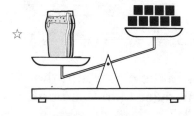

☆ Does the glass weigh more or less than 9 blocks?

more

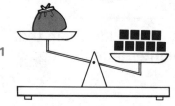

1 Does the purse weigh more or less than 9 blocks?

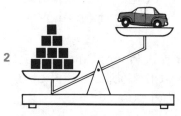

2 Does the car weigh more or less than 10 blocks?

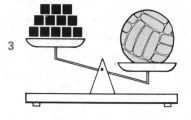

3 Does the ball weigh more or less than 12 blocks?

4 Does the doll weigh more or less than 13 blocks?

B To balance the pans, how many blocks must be added to each **red** pan?

3

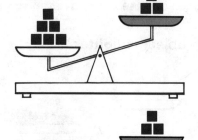

☆

1

2

3

4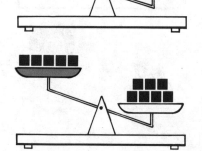

Weight

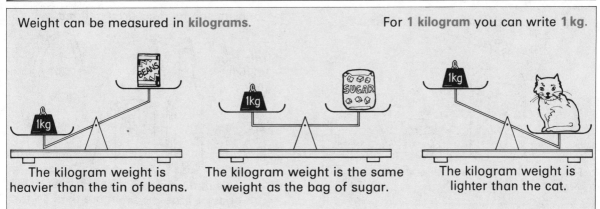

Weight can be measured in **kilograms**.

For **1 kilogram** you can write **1 kg**.

The kilogram weight is heavier than the tin of beans.

The kilogram weight is the same weight as the bag of sugar.

The kilogram weight is lighter than the cat.

A Are these objects heavier or lighter than 1 kilogram?

B Look at the objects below:

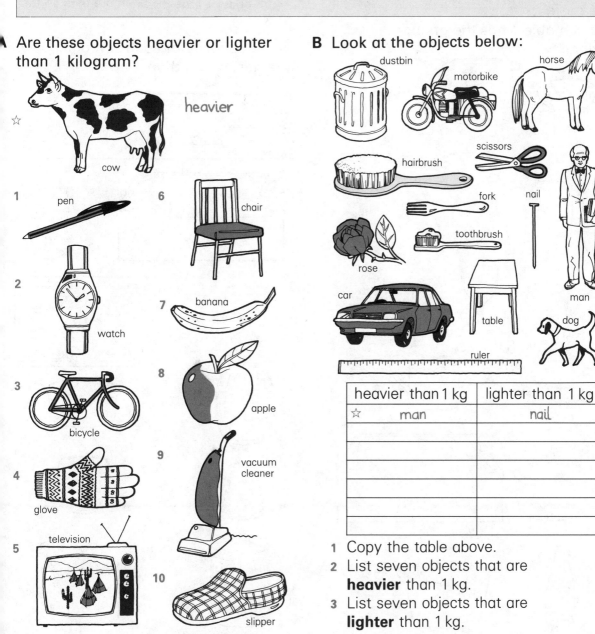

☆ cow — heavier

1 pen

2 watch

3 bicycle

4 glove

5 television

6 chair

7 banana

8 apple

9 vacuum cleaner

10 slipper

dustbin motorbike horse hairbrush scissors fork nail rose toothbrush car table man ruler dog

heavier than 1 kg	lighter than 1 kg
☆ man	nail

1 Copy the table above.
2 List seven objects that are **heavier** than 1 kg.
3 List seven objects that are **lighter** than 1 kg.

The bottle holds more than the glass.

The bottle has the greater **capacity**.

Capacity can be measured in **litres**.

This mug holds less than 1 litre.

This bottle holds about 1 litre.

This bucket holds more than 1 litre.

A Which object has the greater **capacity**?

☆ cup   saucepan   *saucepan*

1   mug   jug

2   cup   glass

3   spoon   mug

4   bowl   bath

5   bottle   saucepan

B Is the capacity of each container greater or less than **1 litre**? *greater*

☆ swimming pool

1   bath

6   glass

2   egg cup

7   fish tank

3   barrel

8   bowl

4   thimble

9   cup

5   dustbin

10   watering can

A Write **red** or **black**:

1 Which is the longer line?

_____

_____

2 Which is the
narrower thumb?

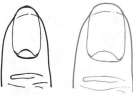

3 Which is the wider string?

B Measure these lines in centimetres:

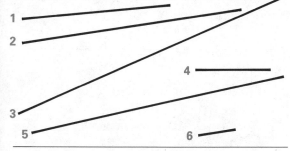

1

2

3

4

5

6

C Draw lines of these lengths:

1 6 cm   5 10 cm

2 9 cm   6 5 cm

3 2 cm   7 3 cm

4 11 cm   8 12 cm

D Measure these lines to the **nearest**
centimetre:

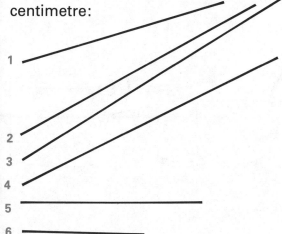

1

2

3

4

5

6

E Which object is **heavier**?

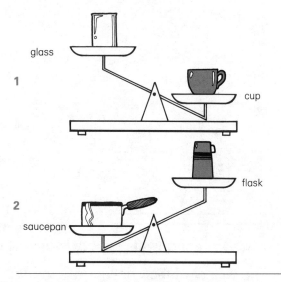

glass

1

cup

2

flask

saucepan

F Do these objects weigh more than
1 kilogram, or less than 1 kilogram?

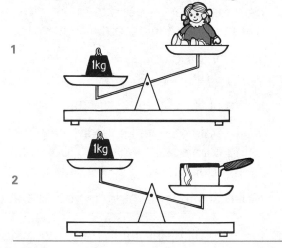

1

1kg

2

1kg

G Which object has the greater
capacity?

1 cup   thimble

2 spoon   glass

3 jam jar   egg cup

A This is a challenge for you and a partner.

Each person collects 5 items which together should weigh less than 1 kilogram.

First check whether the sets of objects weigh more or less than 1 kilogram.

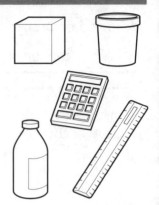

If either person has objects weighing more than 1 kg, that person drops out of the first game.

If both sets of objects weigh less than 1 kilogram, the person whose set of objects is heavier wins the first game.

The winner of the challenge is the first person to win 5 games.

B Find ten different objects in the classroom which together weigh about 1 kilogram. Make of list of your objects.

Now try to balance a 1 kg weight using 9 different objects.

Make of list of these objects.

Try to balance the kilogram weight using 8 objects, then with 7 objects, then 6 objects, and so on until you use only one object.

Make of list of the objects you use each time.

C Find ten different containers in the classroom.

Try to place the containers in order of capacity, smallest first.

Explain how you were able to do this.

Find a way to measure approximately 1 litre of water using only the four smallest containers.

Answer any questions you can. Leave those you cannot do.

1 Which object is heavier, the vase or the glass?

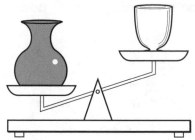

2 Which object is lighter, the train or the car?

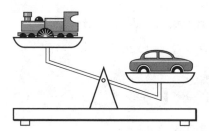

3

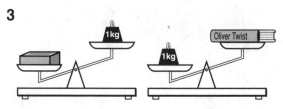

Does the brick weigh more or less than 1 kilogram?

4 Does the book weigh more or less than 1 kg?

5 Does the brick weigh more or less than the book?

Say whether each of the following objects weighs more or less than 1 kg.

6 A bicycle.

7 A chair.

8 A spoon.

9 A dog.

10 On a set of scales, which of these groups of weights would balance 1 kilogram?

Write these weights in grams:

11 1 kg   **12** ½ kg   **13** ¼ kg

Which object has the smaller capacity?

14

15

16 How many full glasses of water are needed to fill the bottle?

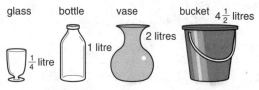

17 How many full glasses of water are needed to fill the vase?

18 Could you fill the glass, the bottle and the vase with one bucket full of water?

19 If the bottle and the glass are filled from a full vase of water, how much water is left in the vase?

20 Write the capacity of the glass in millilitres.

0 1 2 3 4 5 6 7 8 9 10 11 12 13 14 15 16 17 18 19 20

counting in **twos**

A Count in **twos**.
Copy and complete:

☆ 4 ✳ ✳ 10 ✳ ✳ 16

  4 6 8 10 12 14 16

1 0 ✳ 4 6 ✳ 10 12

2 6 ✳ 10 ✳ 14 ✳ 18

3 2 4 ✳ 8 ✳ ✳ 14

4 10 ✳ ✳ 16 ✳ 20 22

5 14 ✳ ✳ ✳ 22 24 ✳

6 20 ✳ ✳ ✳ ✳ ✳ 32

B Use a hundred square.
Finish colouring squares by counting in **twos**:

1	2	3	4	5	6	7	8	9	10
11	12	13	14	15	16	17	18	19	20
21	22	23	24	25	26	27	28	29	30
31	32	33	34	35	36	37	38	39	40
41	42	43	44	45	46	47	48	49	50
51	52	53	54	55	56	57	58	59	60
61	62	63	64	65	66	67	68	69	70
71	72	73	74	75	76	77	78	79	80
81	82	83	84	85	86	87	88	89	90
91	92	93	94	95	96	97	98	99	100

C Copy and complete:

1 The coloured numbers in my square
   are called e — — n numbers.

2 The numbers that are not coloured
   are called o — — numbers.

D Are these numbers **even** or **odd**?

☆ 21   odd

1 6   7 23   13 82

2 9   8 28   14 69

3 5   9 30   15 54

4 1   10 29   16 77

5 12   11 43   17 89

6 17   12 55   18 96

E Count in **twos**. Work out:

☆ How many wheels?   6

1 How many ears?

2 How many legs?

3 How many shoes?

4 How many feet?

5 How many hands?

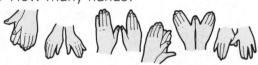

Multiplication

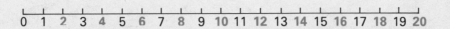

0 1 2 3 4 5 6 7 8 9 10 11 12 13 14 15 16 17 18 19 20

For **2+2+2** write: **2×3**
Say: '2 **multiplied by 3**'

For **2+2+2+2** write: **2×4**
Say: '2 **multiplied by 4**'

For **2×3=6** say:

'2 **multiplied by 3 equals 6**'

For **2×4=8** say:

'2 **multiplied by 4 equals 8**'

Copy and complete:

☆	2+2+2+2+2+2	2×6	12
1	2+2+2		
2	2+2+2+2+2		
3		2×4	
4	2+2		
5	2+2+2+2+2+2+2+2		16
6	2+2+2+2+2+2+2+2+2+2		
7		2×7	
8	2+2+2+2+2+2+2+2+2		

Copy and complete:

☆	2×1=2	2 multiplied by 1 equals 2
1	2×2=4	
2	2×3=✳	
3	2×4=✳	
4		2 multiplied by 5 equals 10
5	2×6=12	
6	2×7=✳	
7		2 multiplied by 8 equals ✳
8	2×9=✳	
9	2×10=✳	

C Multiply to answer these:

☆ How many ears?

$2×4=8$

1 How many eyes?

2 How many wings?

3 How many wheels?

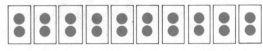

4 How many dots?

☐ ☐ ☐ ☐ ☐ ☐ ☐ ☐

D Multiply to answer these:

☆ How many arms on 6 children? $2×6=12$

1 How many ears on 4 cats?

2 How many feet on 10 ducks?

3 How many legs on 7 geese?

4 How many wings on 5 birds?

5 How many eyes on 9 dolls?

6 How many feet on 2 birds?

7 How many ears on 8 tigers?

8 How many arms on 3 people?

E Write numbers for ✳'s:

☆ 2×2=✳ 4

1 2×5=✳   2×3=✳   7 2×4=✳

2 2×7=✳   5 2×10=✳ 8 2×6=✳

3 2×1=✳   6 2×9=✳   9 2×8=✳

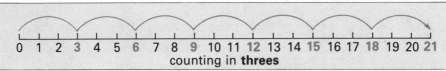

counting in **threes**

A Count in **threes**.
Copy and complete:

☆ 6 ✳ 12 ✳ 18 ✳ 24
  6 9 12 15 18 21 24
1 0 ✳ 6 9 ✳ 15 18
2 3 ✳ 9 ✳ 15 ✳ 21
3 12 ✳ 18 ✳ 24 ✳ 30
4 18 ✳ ✳ 27 ✳ ✳ 36
5 9 ✳ ✳ ✳ ✳ ✳ 27

For **3+3** write: **3×2**.
Say: '3 **multiplied by 2**'

For **3+3+3+3** write: **3×4**
Say: '3 **multiplied by 4**'

For **3×2=6** say:
'**3 multiplied by 2 equals 6**'

For **3×4=12** say:
'**3 multiplied by 4 equals 12**'

B Count in **threes**.
Work out how many:

☆ wheels?

 15

1 soldiers?

2 wheels?

3 dots?

C Use a hundred square.
Finish colouring squares by counting in threes:

1	2	3	4	5	6	7	8	9	10
11	12	13	14	15	16	17	18	19	20
21	22	23	24	25	26	27	28	29	30
31	32	33	34	35	36	37	38	39	40
41	42	43	44	45	46	47	48	49	50
51	52	53	54	55	56	57	58	59	60
61	62	63	64	65	66	67	68	69	70
71	72	73	74	75	76	77	78	79	80
81	82	83	84	85	86	87	88	89	90
91	92	93	94	95	96	97	98	99	100

D Copy and complete:

☆	3+3+3+3	3×4	3 multiplied by 4=12
1	3+3+3+3+3+3		
2		3×10	
3			3 multiplied by 3=9
4		3×8	
5	3+3+3+3+3		
6		3×9	
7			3 multiplied by 7=21

E **Multiply** to answer these.
How many wheels on:

☆ 6 tricycles? 3×6=18
1 8 tricycles?   5 7 tricycles?
2 10 tricycles?   6 3 tricycles?
3 2 tricycles?   7 5 tricycles?
4 9 tricycles?   8 11 tricycles?

F Write numbers for ✳'s:

☆ 3×5=✳   15
1 3×6=✳   5 3×10=✳
2 3×2=✳   6 3×9=✳
3 3×7=✳   7 3×3=✳
4 3×1=✳   8 3×8=✳

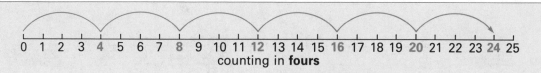

counting in **fours**

Count in **fours**.
Copy and complete:

☆ 8 ✳ 16 ✳ 24 ✳ 32
  8 12 16 20 24 28 32

1 0 ✳ 8 ✳ 16 ✳ 24

2 12 ✳ 20 24 ✳ 32 ✳

3 4 ✳ 12 ✳ 20 ✳ 28

4 16 ✳ ✳ 28 ✳ ✳ 40

5 20 ✳ ✳ ✳ ✳ ✳ 44

Use a hundred square.
Finish colouring squares by counting
in **fours**:

1	2	3	4	5	6	7	8	9	10
11	12	13	14	15	16	17	18	19	20
21	22	23	24	25	26	27	28	29	30
31	32	33	34	35	36	37	38	39	40
41	42	43	44	45	46	47	48	49	50
51	52	53	54	55	56	57	58	59	60
61	62	63	64	65	66	67	68	69	70
71	72	73	74	75	76	77	78	79	80
81	82	83	84	85	86	87	88	89	90
91	92	93	94	95	96	97	98	99	100

Count in **fours**.
Work out how many:

☆ wheels?

 20

1 legs?

2 legs?

3 legs?

For **4+4+4** write: **4×3**
Say: **'4 multiplied by 3'**

For **4+4+4+4** write: **4×4**
Say: **'4 multiplied by 4'**

For **4×3=12** say:
'4 multiplied by 3 equals 12'

For **4×4=16** say:
'4 multiplied by 4 equals 16'

D Multiply to find how many holes:

☆ ⊙⊙⊙⊙⊙ $4 × 5 = 20$

1 ⊙⊙⊙
   ⊙⊙⊙

3 ⊙⊙⊙
   ⊙⊙⊙

2 ⊙⊙⊙⊙
   ⊙⊙⊙⊙

4 ⊙⊙

E Multiply to answer these.
How many legs on:

☆ 6 lions? $4 × 6 = 24$

1 5 deer?   6 4 camels?

2 3 cats?   7 8 sheep?

3 2 dogs?   8 11 cows?

4 7 tigers?   9 9 horses?

5 10 elephants?   10 12 goats?

F Write numbers for ✳'s:

☆ 4×1= ✳   4

1 4×5= ✳   6 4×6= ✳

2 4×7= ✳   7 4×10= ✳

3 4×4= ✳   8 4×3= ✳

4 4×8= ✳   9 4×9= ✳

5 4×2= ✳   10 4×11= ✳

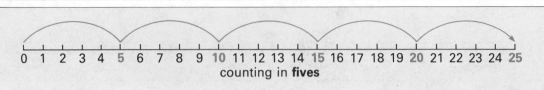

counting in **fives**

A Count in **fives**.
Copy and complete:

☆ 10 ✳ 20 ✳ 30 ✳ 40
    10   15   20   25   30   35   40

1   0 ✳ 10 ✳ 20 ✳ 30

2   15 ✳ 25 ✳ 35 ✳ 45

3   5 ✳ 15 ✳ ✳ 30   35

4   20 ✳ ✳ 35 ✳ ✳ 50

5   35 ✳ ✳ ✳ ✳ ✳ 65

B Use a hundred square.
Finish colouring squares by counting in **fives**:

1	2	3	4	5	6	7	8	9	10
11	12	13	14	15	16	17	18	19	20
21	22	23	24	25	26	27	28	29	30
31	32	33	34	35	36	37	38	39	40
41	42	43	44	45	46	47	48	49	50
51	52	53	54	55	56	57	58	59	60
61	62	63	64	65	66	67	68	69	70
71	72	73	74	75	76	77	78	79	80
81	82	83	84	85	86	87	88	89	90
91	92	93	94	95	96	97	98	99	100

C Count in **fives**.
Work out how many toes:

☆   20

1

2

3

4

5

For **5+5** write: **5×2**
Say: **'5 multiplied by 2'**

For **5+5+5+5** write: **5×4**
Say: **'5 multiplied by 4'**

For **5×2=10** say:
'5 multiplied by 2 equals 10'

For **5×4=20** say:
'5 multiplied by 4 equals 20'

D **Multiply** to find how many legs:

☆   5×3=15

1

2

3

E **Multiply** to answer these:

☆ How many legs on 4 starfish? 5×4=20

1 How many toes on 7 feet?

2 How many legs on 3 starfish?

3 How many toes on 10 feet?

4 How many legs on 8 starfish?

5 How many toes on 5 feet?

F Write numbers for ✳'s:

☆ 5×6= ✳ 30

1   5×2= ✳   6   5×8= ✳

2   5×5= ✳   7   5×1= ✳

3   5×10= ✳   8   5×11= ✳

4   5×7= ✳   9   5×3= ✳

5   5×4= ✳   10   5×9= ✳

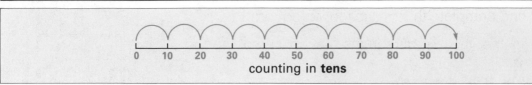

counting in **tens**

Count in **tens**. Copy and complete:

☆ 20 ✳ ✳ 50 ✳ ✳ 80

20 30 40 50 60 70 80

1 0 ✳ 20 30 40 ✳ 60

2 30 ✳ 50 ✳ 70 ✳ 90

3 10 ✳ 30 ✳ ✳ 60 ✳

4 40 ✳ ✳ 70 ✳ ✳ 100

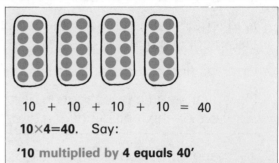

10 + 10 + 10 + 10 = 40

10×4=40. Say:

'10 multiplied by 4 equals 40'

Use a hundred square. Finish
colouring squares by counting
in **tens**:

1	2	3	4	5	6	7	8	9	10
11	12	13	14	15	16	17	18	19	20
21	22	23	24	25	26	27	28	29	30
31	32	33	34	35	36	37	38	39	40
41	42	43	44	45	46	47	48	49	50
51	52	53	54	55	56	57	58	59	60
61	62	63	64	65	66	67	68	69	70
71	72	73	74	75	76	77	78	79	80
81	82	83	84	85	86	87	88	89	90
91	92	93	94	95	96	97	98	99	100

D Multiply to find how many toes:

☆

10×4=40

1

2

Count in **tens**.
Work out how many pencils:

☆

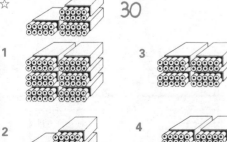

30

1   3

2   4

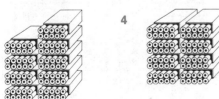

E Multiply to find how many pence:

☆

10×5=50

1

2

3

F Write numbers for ✳'s:

☆ 10×3= ✳ 30

1 10×6= ✳   4 10×7= ✳   7 10×10= ✳

2 10×4= ✳   5 10×9= ✳   8 10×2= ✳

3 10×1= ✳   6 10×5= ✳   9 10×8= ✳

A Copy and complete this multiplication square.

Add together the numbers in the first column of the red square.

1 + 2 + 3 + 4 = 10

Add together the numbers in each of the next 3 columns. Use a calculator if you need to.

Can you find any pattern in these totals?

Now try the same investigation using other squares of numbers on the multiplication square.

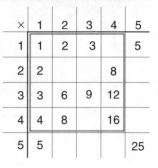

×	1	2	3	4	5
1	1	2	3		5
2	2			8	
3	3	6	9	12	
4	4	8		16	
5	5				25

B You need some copies of this circle.

Write down the multiples of 3 up to 3 × 10
...3 6 9 12 15...

Now write down the last figure in each multiple
...3 6 9 2 5...

Draw a straight line on your circle from the first number you have written ...3 to the next number ...6.

From 6, draw another straight line to the next number ...9.

Continue in this way joining all of the numbers in turn. What do you discover?

Use another circle and try this investigation with the multiples of 2. What do you find?

Try the investigation with multiples of 4, 5 and 10.

C Write down the multiples of 4 up to 4 × 10.

4   8   12   16   20.......

Add together the figures in each multiple until you have a single figure.

1+2 1+6 2+0

4   8   3   7   2.......

You can now use these figures to form a pattern.

On squared paper draw a line 4 sections long. Turn right and draw a line 8 sections long. Turn right and draw a line 3 sections long. Carry on in this way using the numbers you have found.

Try to form patterns in this way using the multiples of other numbers.

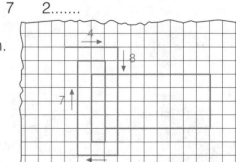

Answer any questions you can. Leave those you cannot do.
Do not use a calculator for any of the questions.

Write down the missing numbers.

1 2 4 6 ✳ 10 12

2 3 6 ✳ 12 15 ✳

3 4 ✳ 12 16 ✳ 24

4 10 15 ✳ 25 30 ✳

5 16 20 24 ✳ ✳ 36

6 18 ✳ 24 ✳ 30 33

Choose the multiplication you would use to answer these questions:

7 How many legs on ten people?

  4 × 10   2 × 5   2 × 10

8 How many wheels on 8 cars?

  8 × 2   4 × 8   8 × 8

9 How many toes on 7 children?

  7 × 7   10 × 5   10 × 7

10 How many wheels on 5 tricycles?

11 How many legs on nine giraffes?

12 How many shoes in 7 pairs?

13 How many toes on ten feet?

Are these numbers odd or even?

14 6

15 24

16 47

17 91

18 103

Write numbers for ✳'s

19 2 × 8 = ✳

20 10 × 5 = ✳

21 3 × 7 = ✳

22 2 × 6 = ✳

23 4 × 10 = ✳

24 3 × 4 = ✳

25 10 × 10 = ✳

26 ✳ × 7 = 28

27 3 × 8 = ✳

28 5 × 5 = ✳

29 ✳ × 10 = 30

30 5 × 6 = ✳

31 2 × ✳ = 18

32 4 × 6 = ✳

33 5 × ✳ = 45

34 4 × 8 = ✳

35 10 × 7 = ✳

36 ✳ × 5 = 20

37 10 × 8 = ✳

38 5 × 9 = ✳

39 10 × 3 = ✳

40 5 × 4 = ✳

41 7 × 3 = ✳

42 8 × ✳ = 64

43 9 × ✳ = 45

44 ✳ × 6 = 42

45 ✳ × 3 = 18

46 9 × 9 = ✳

47 7 × ✳ = 49

48 6 × 7 = ✳

49 8 × ✳ = 48

50 ✳ × 8 = 56

51 18 × 10 = ✳

52 123 × 10 = ✳

53 26 × 100 = ✳

54 1 3
   × 6
   ✳✳

55 1 4 3
   × 4
   ✳✳✳

A How many each if:

☆ the spiders catch an equal number of flies? *3*

1 each man has the same number of dogs?

2 the dogs catch an equal number of cats?

3 the men have an equal number of birds?

4 each man has the same number of cats?

5 the birds eat an equal number of worms?

6 the cats catch an equal number of mice?

B How many each if you:

☆ share the flies equally among 6 spiders? *2*

1 share the worms equally among 6 birds?

2 share the cats equally among 4 men?

3 share the mice equally among 3 cats?

4 share the flies equally among 3 spiders?

5 share the birds equally among 3 men?

6 share the worms equally among 2 birds?

C How many each if you:

☆ share these dummies equally among 3 babies? *2*

1 share these sweets equally among 4 children?

2 share these coins equally between 2 children?

3 share these balls equally between 5 children?

4 share these carrots equally among 3 rabbits?

5 share these coins equally among 3 children?

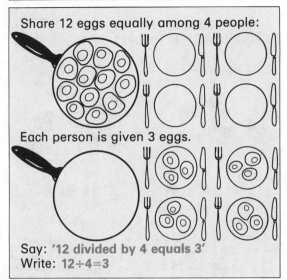

Share 12 eggs equally among 4 people:

Each person is given 3 eggs.

Say: '12 divided by 4 equals 3'
Write: **12÷4=3**

Share these **12** counters into **3** equal groups:

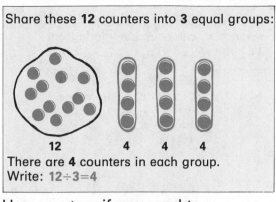

12   4   4   4

There are **4** counters in each group.
Write: **12÷3=4**

Write these answers in 2 different ways:

☆ Share 10 sausages equally between 2 children:

10 divided by 2 = 5
10÷2=5

1 Share 15 eggs equally among 5 people:

2 Share 12 pieces of bacon equally among 3 people:

3 Share 8 sausages equally among 4 people:

4 Share 20 mushrooms equally among 5 people:

B Use counters if you need to.
Share these counters into:

☆ 2 equal groups

$8÷2=4$

1 3 equal groups

2 2 equal groups

3 4 equal groups

4 5 equal groups

5 3 equal groups

6 10 equal groups

C Use counters if you need to.
Copy and complete:

☆ 6÷2= ✳ $6÷2=3$

1 10÷2= ✳   4 18÷3= ✳   7 16÷4= ✳

2 8÷4= ✳   5 20÷10= ✳   8 25÷5= ✳

3 10÷5= ✳   6 21÷3= ✳   9 20÷4= ✳

Apples are packed in **fours**.
How many packs can be made from
12 apples?

After 1 pack is made, **8 apples** are left:

After 2 packs are made, **4 apples** are left:

After 3 packs are made, **no apples** are left!

0 1 2 3 4 5 6 7 8 9 10 11 12

3 groups of 4 can be subtracted from 12.
3 **packs** can be made.

How many groups of **3** can you
make from these counters:

15 counters

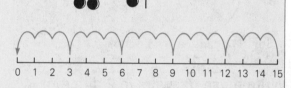

0 1 2 3 4 5 6 7 8 9 10 11 12 13 14 15

5 groups of 3 can be subtracted from 15.
5 **groups** can be made.

A Find how many packs
can be made when:

☆ these apples are packed in **threes**:

    5

1 these apples are packed in **twos**:

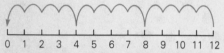

2 these tomatoes are packed in **fives**:

3 these oranges are packed in **fours**:

4 these plums are packed in **threes**:

5 these onions are packed in **twos**:

B Use counters if you need to.
Find how many groups
can be made when:

☆ these counters are in groups of 4:

 3 groups

1 these counters are in groups of 2:

2 these counters are in groups of 3:

3 these counters are in groups of 5:

4 these counters are in groups of 4:

5 these counters are in groups of 10:

6 these counters are in groups of 5:

How many groups of **2** can you make from **10**?

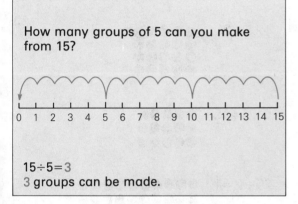

0 1 2 3 4 5 6 7 8 9 10

5 groups of 2 can be subtracted from 10.
5 groups can be made.
Say: **'10 divided by 2 equals 5'**
Write: **10÷2=5**

How many groups of 5 can you make from 15?

0 1 2 3 4 5 6 7 8 9 10 11 12 13 14 15

15÷5=3
3 groups can be made.

Use a number line if you need to.

☆ How many groups of 2 can be made from 8? $8÷2=4$ 4 groups

1 How many groups of 2 can be made from 12?

2 How many groups of 3 can be made from 18?

3 How many groups of 4 can be made from 20?

4 How many groups of 5 can be made from 25?

5 How many groups of 10 can be made from 30?

6 How many groups of 4 can be made from 28?

7 How many groups of 3 can be made from 27?

8 How many groups of 2 can be made from 20?

B Use division to answer these:

☆ Apples are packed in fours. How many packs can be made with 20 apples?  $20÷4=5$
5 packs

1 Onions are packed in threes. How many packs can be made with 21 onions?

2 Bananas are sold in bunches of 4. How many bunches can be made with 40 bananas?

3 Sweets cost 2p each. How many can you buy with 20p?

4 Balls are packed in tens. How many packs can be made with 70 balls?

5 Lollies cost 10p. How many lollies can you buy with 90p?

6 Felt pens are packed in fives. How many packs can be made with 35 pens?

7 Oranges are packed in threes. How many packs can be made with 30 oranges?

8 Pencils cost 5p. How many pencils can you buy with 45p?

C Use a number line if you need to. Write numbers for ✳'s:

☆ $20÷4=$✳   5

1 $16÷2=$✳   6 $25÷5=$✳

2 $18÷3=$✳   7 $40÷10=$✳

3 $15÷5=$✳   8 $50÷10=$✳

4 $24÷4=$✳   9 $32÷4=$✳

5 $30÷10=$✳   10 $100÷10=$✳

This pattern of 12 counters shows that:

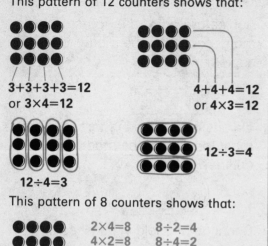

3+3+3+3=12
or 3×4=12

4+4+4=12
or 4×3=12

12÷3=4

12÷4=3

This pattern of 8 counters shows that:

2×4=8   8÷2=4
4×2=8   8÷4=2

If you know that **3×5=15**
you can write 3 more facts:

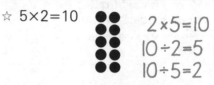

5×3=15
15÷3=5
15÷5=3

A Write numbers for ✳'s:

☆ 3×2= ✳ 6
  2×3= ✳ 6
  6÷2= ✳ 3
  6÷ ✳ =2 3

1 5×3= ✳
   3×5= ✳
   15÷3= ✳
   15÷5= ✳

2 4×5= ✳
   5× ✳ =20
   20÷ ✳ =5
   20÷ ✳ =4

3 4×2= ✳
   2×4= ✳
   8÷4= ✳
   8÷ ✳ =4

4 2×10= ✳
   10× ✳ =20
   20÷ ✳ =10
   20÷ ✳ =2

5 3×3= ✳
   ✳ ÷3=3

B Write 3 more facts for each of these:

☆ 5×2=10

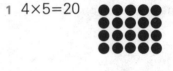

2×5=10
10÷2=5
10÷5=2

1 4×5=20

2 5×3=15

3 20÷2=10

4 18÷3=6

C Use counters if you need to.
Write numbers for ✳'s:

☆ 5×4=20
  4×5= ✳   20
  20÷ ✳ =5   4
  20÷ ✳ =4   5

1 2×6=12
   6×2= ✳
   ✳ ÷2=6
   ✳ ÷6=2

2 4×3=12
   3× ✳ =12
   12÷ ✳ =3
   ✳ ÷3=4

3 10×3=30
   3× ✳ =30
   ✳ ÷10=3
   30÷ ✳ =10

4 10×5=50
   5× ✳ =50
   50÷ ✳ =5
   50÷ ✳ =10

A Are these numbers even or odd?

1 17	6 14	11 40
2 24	7 11	12 107
3 32	8 3	13 65
4 60	9 99	14 112
5 71	10 66	15 200

B Copy and complete:

1	4+4+4+4+4	4×5	
2		3×7	21
3	5+5+5+5+5		25
4		2×8	
5	10+10+10+10+10+10+10		
6		5×7	
7		10×6	
8		2×9	
9	3+3+3+3+3+3+3+3		
10		5×9	
11		4×7	
12	4+4+4+4+4+4+4+4		

C Write numbers for ✶'s:

1 2×7=✶	13 10×5=✶
2 4×6=✶	14 2×6=✶
3 3×8=✶	15 4×9=✶
4 10×9=✶	16 5×9=✶
5 2×9=✶	17 3×6=✶
6 4×4=✶	18 4×7=✶
7 3×9=✶	19 5×8=✶
8 2×11=✶	20 2×5=✶
9 4×8=✶	21 10×10=✶
10 3×7=✶	22 4×11=✶
11 5×5=✶	23 5×7=✶
12 3×10=✶	24 3×3=✶

D How many each when:

1 24 fish are divided equally among 3 fishermen?

2 27 sweets are divided equally among 3 children?

3 50 worms are shared equally among 5 birds?

4 18 flies are shared equally between 2 spiders?

E How many packs when:

1 18 apples are packed in twos?

2 27 apples are packed in threes?

3 40 apples are packed in fours?

4 100 apples are packed in tens?

5 45 apples are packed in fives?

6 24 apples are packed in threes?

7 36 apples are packed in fours?

F Write numbers for ✶'s:

1 12÷2=✶	9 60÷10=✶
2 20÷2=✶	10 40÷10=✶
3 15÷3=✶	11 16÷2=✶
4 27÷3=✶	12 6÷3=✶
5 40÷4=✶	13 18÷3=✶
6 16÷4=✶	14 28÷4=✶
7 25÷5=✶	15 36÷4=✶
8 40÷5=✶	16 100÷10=✶

G Write numbers for ✶'s:

1 3×5=✶	7 40÷10=✶
2 5×3=✶	8 40÷4=✶
3 15÷5=✶	9 4×5=✶
4 15÷3=✶	10 5×4=✶
5 4×10=✶	11 20÷5=✶
6 10×4=✶	12 20÷4=✶

A Copy this table with ticks to show when each number can be divided into equal groups.

Number	1	2	3	4	5	6	7	8	9	10	11
Can be divided into 2 equal groups		✓		✓		✓		✓		✓	
Can be divided into 3 equal groups			✓			✓			✓		
Can be divided into 4 equal groups				✓				✓			
Can be divided into 5 equal groups					✓					✓	
Can be divided into 10 equal groups										✓	

Continue the table beyond the number 11 until you find a number that can be divided into 2, 3, 5 and 10 equal groups.

B With 12 apples, how many groups of 5 can you make and how many apples will be left over?

You can work this out on a calculator by continuing to take away 5 until there is less than 5 left.

| 12 | − 5 | = 7 | − 5 | = 2 |

2 groups of 5 can be made. 2 apples are left over.

Use a calculator to work out:

1 how many groups of 3 cakes you can make with 22 cakes and how many cakes are left over.

2 how many packs of 10 pies you can make with 48 pies and how many pies are left over.

3 how many groups of 5 children you can make with 40 children and how many children are left over.

C A pie maker makes 100 pies each day.

He can pack the pies in boxes of 3 4 5 6 7 8 or 9

He wants no pies left over if possible.

What size boxes can the pieman use?

Answer any questions you can. Leave those you cannot do.

How many each when:

1 16 worms are shared equally among 4 birds?

2 30 carrots are shared equally among 5 people?

3 40 mushrooms are shared equally among 10 people?

4 £18 is shared equally between 2 people?

How many groups can be made when:

5 these counters are put into groups of 3?

6 these counters are put into groups of 5?

How many packs when:

7 28 sweets are packed in fours?

8 35 plums are packed in fives?

9 80 lollies are packed in tens?

10 27 oranges are packed in threes?

11 Stickers cost 5p. How many stickers can you buy if you have 35p?

12 Biscuits cost 4p each. How many biscuits can you buy with 32p?

13 Sweets cost 3p. How many sweets can you buy with 15p?

Write numbers for $*$'s

14 $12 \div 3 = *$

15 $50 \div 10 = *$

16 $25 \div 5 = *$

17 $8 \div 4 = *$

18 $21 \div 3 = *$

19 $70 \div 10 = *$

20 $15 \div 5 = *$

21 $28 \div 4 = *$

22 $18 \div * = 9$

23 $40 \div * = 10$

24 $40 \div 5 = *$

25 $32 \div 4 = *$

26 $* \div 5 = 10$

27 $* \div 5 = 4$

28 $35 \div * = 7$

29 $* \div 10 = 3$

30 $* \div 3 = 8$

31 $28 \div 7 = *$

32 $36 \div 6 = *$

33 $48 \div 8 = *$

34 $* \div 5 = 7$

35 $32 \div * = 4$

36 $130 \div 10 = *$

37 $400 \div 10 = *$

38 $* \div 10 = 26$

39 $800 \div 100 = *$

40 $1200 \div 100 = *$

Write answers for these divisions.

41 $4 \overline{)64}$

42 $7 \overline{)91}$

43 $5 \overline{)355}$

44 $8 \overline{)464}$

Work out the answer and the remainder for these divisions

45 $4 \overline{)57}$

46 $2 \overline{)353}$

47 $6 \overline{)527}$

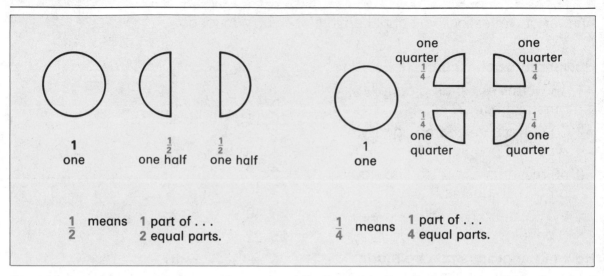

A Copy these shapes on squared paper. Colour $\frac{1}{2}$ of each shape:	**B** Copy these shapes on squared paper. Colour $\frac{1}{4}$ of each shape:

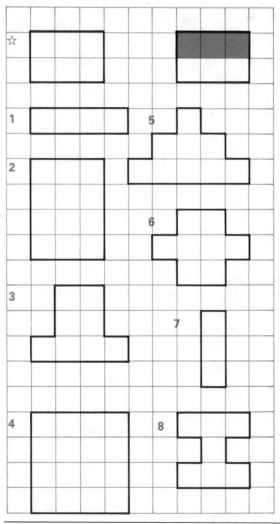 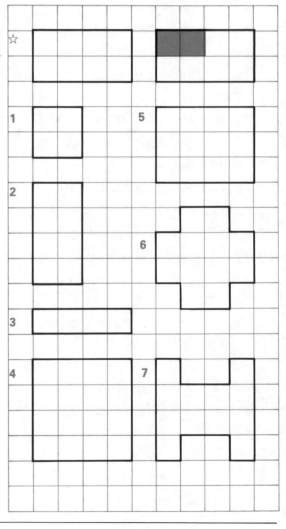

Fractions

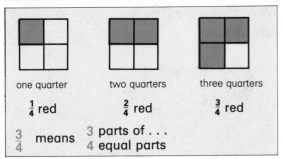

one quarter — $\frac{1}{4}$ red   two quarters — $\frac{2}{4}$ red   three quarters — $\frac{3}{4}$ red

$\frac{3}{4}$ means 3 parts of . . . 4 equal parts

What fraction of each shape is red?

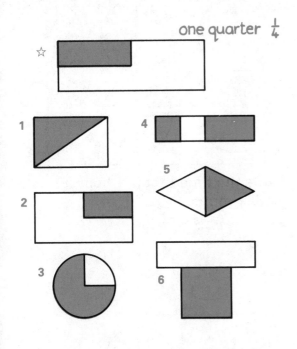

one quarter $\frac{1}{4}$

1

2

3

4

5

6

C What fraction of each shape is **black**, and what fraction is **red**?

black $\frac{1}{4}$ red $\frac{1}{2}$

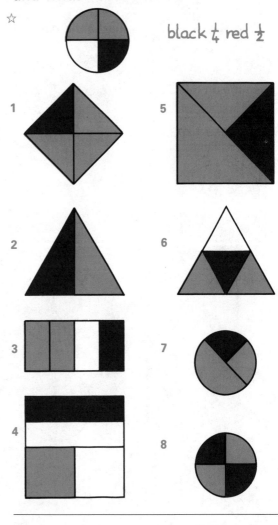

1   5

2   6

3   7

4   8

Copy these on squared paper.
Colour the fraction shown:

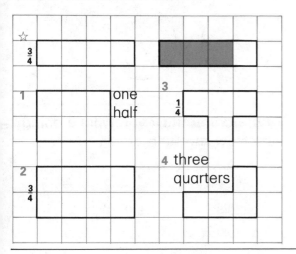

$\frac{3}{4}$

1   one half

3   $\frac{1}{4}$

2   $\frac{3}{4}$

4 three quarters

D How many whole oranges will give:

6 halves?   3

1   10 halves?   6   8 quarters?

2   12 halves?   7   12 quarters?

3   4 quarters?   8   2 halves?

4   16 halves?   9   16 quarters?

5   20 halves?   10   40 halves?

The long hand is the **minute** hand.
The short hand is the **hour** hand.

The time on this clock is 5 o'clock.

A Write these times:

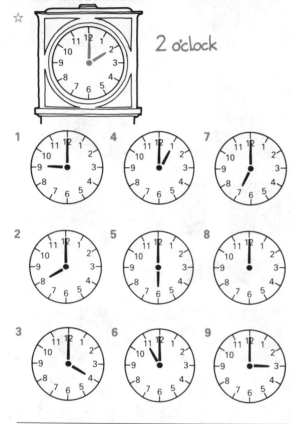

☆ 2 o'clock

1

4

7

2

5

8

3

6

9

B Use clock faces to show these times.

☆ 10 o'clock:

1 1 o'clock
2 7 o'clock
3 9 o'clock
4 11 o'clock
5 6 o'clock
6 8 o'clock
7 3 o'clock
8 5 o'clock
9 12 o'clock

C Write the time that is 1 hour **later** than:

☆

6 o'clock

1

3

5

2

4

6

D Write the time that is 1 hour **earlier** than:

☆

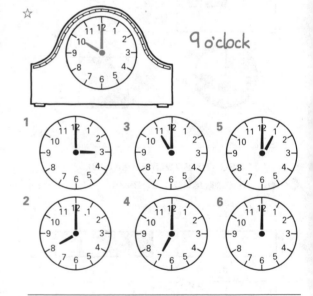

9 o'clock

1

3

5

2

4

6

E What do you think you will be doing tomorrow morning at:

☆ 2 o'clock? sleeping
1 10 o'clock?
2 6 o'clock?
3 9 o'clock?
4 8 o'clock?
5 5 o'clock?
6 11 o'clock?

Time

 The time on this clock is **half past four**.

The **minute** hand is half way round.

The **hour** hand is between the 8 and the 9.

Half an hour **earlier** the time was **four o'clock**:

The time on this clock is **half past 8**.

 Half an hour **later** the time will be **five o'clock**.

Write these times:

☆  half past four

1	4	7

2	5	8

3	6	9

Draw clock faces to show these times:

☆ half past 2

1 half past 8	6 half past 9
2 half past 11	7 half past 10
3 half past 6	8 half past 12
4 half past 1	9 half past 3
5 half past 5	

C Use a clock face if you need to.
Write the time that is half an hour **earlier** than:

☆   9 o'clock

1	2	3

D Write the time that is half an hour **later** than:

☆  6 o'clock

1	3	5

2	4	6

The **minute** hand is one quarter way round.

The **hour** hand is just past the 10.

The time on this clock is: $\frac{1}{4}$ past ten.

  The time on this clock is **quarter past seven**.

$\frac{1}{4}$ of an hour **earlier** the time was **seven o'clock**:

 $\frac{1}{4}$ of an hour **later** the time will be **half past seven**.

A Write these times:

 $\frac{1}{4}$ past 5

1   **4**   **7**

2   **5**   **8**

3   **6**   **9**

B Use clock faces to show these times:

☆ $\frac{1}{4}$ past 8

1 $\frac{1}{4}$ past 7   4 $\frac{1}{4}$ past 4   7 $\frac{1}{4}$ past 2
2 $\frac{1}{4}$ past 6   5 $\frac{1}{4}$ past 1   8 $\frac{1}{4}$ past 11
3 $\frac{1}{4}$ past 3   6 $\frac{1}{4}$ past 10   9 $\frac{1}{4}$ past 12

C Use a clock face if you need to. Write the time that is $\frac{1}{4}$ hour **earlier** than:

☆ 10 o'clock

1   **3**   **5**

2   **4**   **6**

D Write the time that is $\frac{1}{4}$ hour **later** than:

☆  half past one

1    **2**   **3**

The time on this clock is **quarter to three**.

The minute hand still has a quarter to turn. The hour hand is nearly on the 3.

  The time on this clock is **quarter to five**.

$\frac{1}{4}$ of an hour **earlier** the time was half past four:

$\frac{1}{4}$ of an hour **later** the time will be five o'clock.

Write these times:

☆ 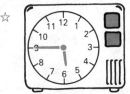 quarter to six

1

4

7

2

5

8

3

6

9

Use clock faces to show these times:

☆ $\frac{1}{4}$ to 7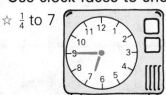

1 $\frac{1}{4}$ to 8   **4** $\frac{1}{4}$ to 6   **7** $\frac{1}{4}$ to 3

2 $\frac{1}{4}$ to 10   **5** $\frac{1}{4}$ to 1   **8** $\frac{1}{4}$ to 5

3 $\frac{1}{4}$ to 12   **6** $\frac{1}{4}$ to 9   **9** $\frac{1}{4}$ to 11

C Use a clock face if you need to. Write the time that is $\frac{1}{4}$ hour **earlier** than:

☆ 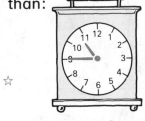 half past one

1

2

3

D Write the time that is $\frac{1}{4}$ hour **later** than:

 11 o'clock

☆

1

3

5

2

4

6

You need 12 clock faces stamped in your book.
Draw hands on your clock faces to show each of these times for Jimmy:

1   Wakes up

half past seven

2   Washes

quarter to eight

3   Eats breakfast

quarter past eight

4   Arrives at school

quarter to nine

5   Starts maths lesson

half past nine

6   Told off by teacher

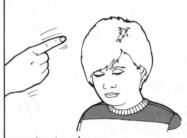

quarter to eleven

7   Falls over in playground

quarter past twelve

8   Starts lunch

half past twelve

9   Leaves school

four o'clock

10   Goes to play with friend

quarter to five

11   Told off by mum

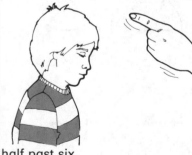

half past six

12   Goes to bed

eight o'clock

A What fraction of each shape is red?

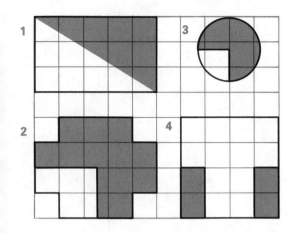

B How many whole apples will give:

1 4 halves?   6 16 halves?
2 8 halves?   7 16 quarters?
3 4 quarters?   8 20 halves?
4 10 halves?   9 14 halves?
5 12 quarters?   10 8 quarters?

C Write these times:

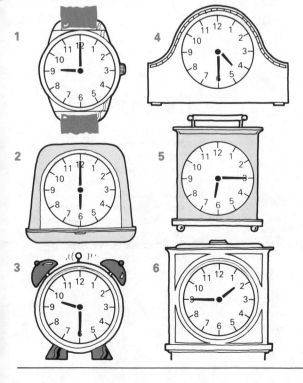

D Use clock faces to show these times:

1 7 o'clock   6 $\frac{1}{4}$ past nine
2 3 o'clock   7 $\frac{1}{4}$ past two
3 10 o'clock   8 $\frac{1}{4}$ to ten
4 $\frac{1}{2}$ past four   9 $\frac{1}{4}$ to twelve
5 $\frac{1}{2}$ past eleven 10 $\frac{1}{4}$ past six

E Write the time that is 1 hour earlier than:

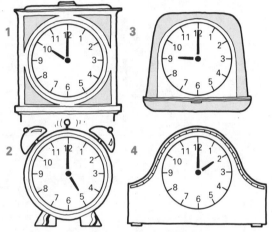

F Write the time that is half an hour later than:

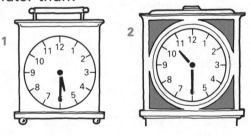

G Write the time that is $\frac{1}{4}$ hour earlier than:

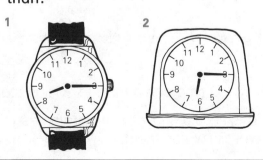

A Copy the diagram below.

Draw pictures and matching clock faces to tell the story of your day.

The pictures must be in order, so Picture 2 must show something that happened after you woke up and before you left for school.

B You need a copy of the television programmes for one day.

Choose one of the channels.

Draw a time chain for this channel.

Here is an example:

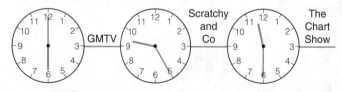

ITV London

6.00	GMTV
9.25	Scratchy & Co
11.30	The Chart Show
12.30	Mad Science
1.00	News & Weather
1.05	London Today
1.10	Movies, Games and Videos
1.40	James and the Giant Peach
2.10	Airwolf
3.00	Thunder in Paradise
3.55	RoboCop

Draw a time chain for a television station of your own.

This should show the programmes you enjoy at the time you want to watch them.

Answer any questions you can. Leave those you cannot do.

Write the time shown on each clock below:

1

2

3

4

5

6

7

Use clock faces to show these times:

8 10 o'clock

9 $\frac{1}{2}$ past 4

10 quarter past nine

11 quarter to 2

12 10 past 7

13 20 to 9

Write the time that is:

14 1 hour earlier than 4 o'clock

15 1 hour later than $\frac{1}{2}$ past 10

16 $\frac{1}{2}$ hour earlier than 6 o'clock

17 $\frac{1}{2}$ hour earlier than half past 1

18 $\frac{1}{4}$ hour later than 3 o'clock

19 $\frac{1}{4}$ hour earlier than $\frac{1}{2}$ past 11

20 $\frac{1}{4}$ hour earlier than 12 o'clock

21 $\frac{1}{4}$ hour later than $\frac{1}{4}$ to 4

Write the time shown on each clock below:

22

23

24

25

Use clock faces to show these times:

26 10 to 7

27 25 past 9

28 20 to 11

29 5 past 6

30 25 to 1

31 20 past 2

Here is a line of 6 counters: ●●●●●●

Here is a line of 4 counters: ●●●●

There are **2 more** counters on the top line. The **difference** between the lines is 2 counters. You can use **subtraction** to find the **difference**.

Write: **6−4=2**

A What is the **difference** between these lines of counters?

☆ ●●●●●●
　 ●●●　　　　　　4 counters

1 ●●●●●●●
　 ●●●●●

2 ●●●●●●
　 ●●●●●

3 ●●●●●●●●
　 ●●●●●

4 ●●●●●●●●●●
　 ●●●●●

5 ●●●●●●●
　 ●●●●

6 ●●●●●●●●●●●
　 ●●●●

7 ●●●●●●●●●
　 ●●

B Use counters if you need to. Work out the **difference** between:

☆ 5 and 9　●●●●●
　　　　　　●●●●●●●●●　　4

1 6 and 8　　　　5 3 and 10

2 3 and 7　　　　6 2 and 11

3 2 and 8　　　　7 6 and 12

4 4 and 9　　　　8 4 and 12

C Use subtraction to find how many more **black** counters than **red** counters:

☆ 　　　　　　　10−6=4

1 　　　　　4

2 　　　　　5

3 　　　　　6

D Use subtraction to find the **difference** between:

☆ 5 and 11　11−5=6

1 2 and 8　　5 11 and 4　　9 2 and 10

2 4 and 9　　6 6 and 13　　10 1 and 14

3 12 and 5　7 15 and 6　　11 3 and 17

4 9 and 7　　8 13 and 8　　12 5 and 20

E Use subtraction to find how many years **difference** in age if:

☆ John is 9 and Ann is 7　9−7=2

1 Bill is 10 and Jane is 6

2 Paula is 11 and Bob is 5

3 Jo is 9 and Jill is 2

4 Fred is 6 and Mike is 12

5 Alan is 7 and his brother is 18

6 Jess is 5 and her sister is 15

7 Anna is 8 and Sarah is 10

8 Trevor is 4 and Sue is 17

9 Joan is 19 and Max is 10

10 Sally is 6 and Lisa is 11

Subtraction

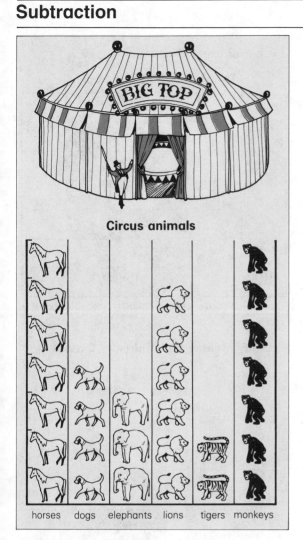

Circus animals

| horses | dogs | elephants | lions | tigers | monkeys |

A Use the graph to find how many:

☆ dogs 4

1 elephants 3 horses 5 tigers

2 lions 4 monkeys

B Use the graph to answer these:

☆ How many more lions than dogs? 2

1 How many more horses than elephants?

2 How many more monkeys than lions?

3 How many more lions than tigers?

4 How many more monkeys than dogs?

5 How many animals altogether?

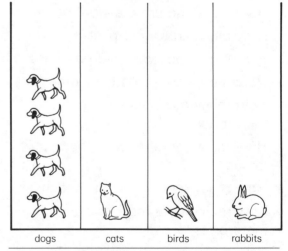

C Copy and complete this **picture graph** for John's pets:

John's pets

| dogs | cats | birds | rabbits |

D Use your **picture graph** to answer these:

☆ How many more birds than cats? 3

1 How many more dogs than cats?

2 How many more birds than dogs?

3 How many more rabbits than cats?

4 How many pets altogether?

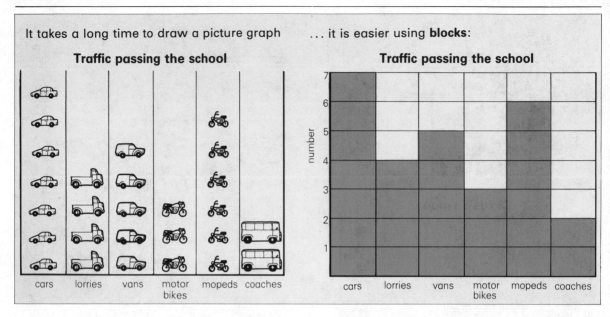

It takes a long time to draw a picture graph

Traffic passing the school

... it is easier using **blocks**:

Traffic passing the school

A Use the **block graph** to answer these:

☆ How many vans went past? 5

1 How many lorries went past?

2 How many coaches went past?

3 How many motorbikes went past?

4 How many cars went past?

5 How many mopeds went past?

6 How many more cars than lorries?

7 How many more vans than motorbikes?

8 How many more mopeds than lorries?

9 How many more cars than coaches?

10 How many more mopeds than motorbikes?

11 How many mopeds and motorbikes altogether?

12 How many coaches and lorries altogether?

13 How many cars and vans altogether?

14 How many fewer coaches than lorries?

15 How many fewer vans than cars?

Birthday months for children in Class 3

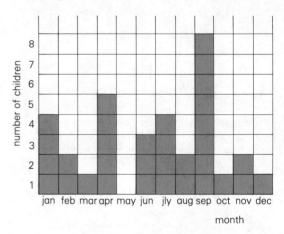

month

B How many children had birthdays in:

☆ July? 4

1 April?   4 June?   7 November?

2 December? 5 March?   8 January?

3 February? 6 October? 9 May?

C Use the **block graph** to answer these.

1 Which month had most birthdays?

2 Which month had fewest birthdays?

3 How many birthdays altogether in January, February, March and April?

4 How many children in Class 3?

Subtraction

A The children in Class 3 were asked to name their favourite fruits.
This table shows their answers:

favourite fruit	apple	orange	banana	pear	plum
number of children	8	6	4	7	8

Copy and complete this block graph:

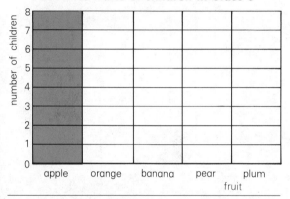

Favourite fruits of children in Class 3

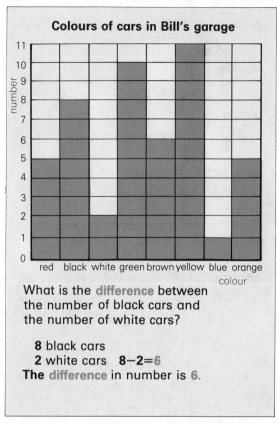

Colours of cars in Bill's garage

What is the **difference** between the number of black cars and the number of white cars?

8 black cars
2 white cars   **8−2=6**
The difference in number is **6**.

B The children in Class 3 were asked to name their favourite colours.
This table shows their answers:

favourite colour	red	blue	green	yellow	orange	purple
number of children	6	5	2	7	1	7

Copy and complete this block graph:

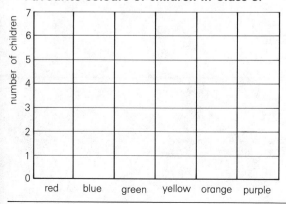

Favourite colours of children in Class 3.

C What is the difference between:

☆ the number of yellow cars and the number of blue cars?   **11−1=10**

1 the number of green cars and the number of brown cars?

2 the number of yellow cars and the number of orange cars?

3 the number of black cars and the number of blue cars?

4 the number of yellow cars and the number of green cars?

5 the number of orange cars and the number of white cars?

6 the number of yellow cars and the number of black cars?

7 the number of green cars and the number of red cars?

8 the number of black cars and the number of brown cars?

Sharon **estimated** (guessed) that the length of this line was 5 cm.
Then she **measured** the line. She found it was 7 cm long.

estimate: **5** cm   measure: **7** cm

The difference between the estimate and the measure was **7 cm − 5 cm = 2 cm**

A Copy this table. Do not fill it in yet:

spider	estimate	measure	difference
1	cm	cm	cm
2	cm	cm	cm
3	cm	cm	cm
4	cm	cm	cm
5	cm	cm	cm
6	cm	cm	cm
7	cm	cm	cm
8	cm	cm	cm
9	cm	cm	cm
10	cm	cm	cm

B 1 Estimate how far spider 1 has dropped. Write your estimate in the table.

  2 Measure how far spider 1 has dropped. Write your measure in the table.

  3 Work out the difference between your estimate and the measure. Write your answer in the table.

  4 Do the same for the other spiders.

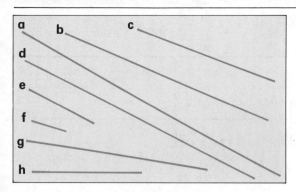

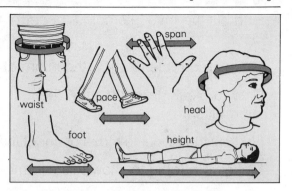

Copy this table. Do not fill it in yet:

line	estimate	measure	difference
a	cm	cm	cm
b	cm	cm	cm
c	cm	cm	cm
d	cm	cm	cm
e	cm	cm	cm
f	cm	cm	cm
g	cm	cm	cm
h	cm	cm	cm

1 Estimate the length of line **a**.

2 Measure the length of line **a**.

3 Work out the difference between your estimate and the measure.

4 Write your answers in the table.

5 Do the same for the other lines.

How long altogether?

☆ line **d**+line **e** $7cm + 2cm = 9cm$

1 line **a**+line **g**   4 line **a**+line **b**+line **d**

2 line **b**+line **h**   5 line **d**+line **g**+line **h**

3 line **c**+line **d**   6 line **a**+line **c**+line **h**

What is the **difference** in length between these lines?

☆ line **b** and line **g** $6cm - 5cm = 1cm$

1 line **b** and line **e**   4 line **e** and line **g**

2 line **f** and line **h**   5 line **h** and line **c**

3 line **d** and line **f**   6 line **c** and line **f**

E Copy and complete this table:

distance	estimate	measure	difference
Your span	cm	cm	cm
Length of your foot	cm	cm	cm
Your pace	cm	cm	cm
Around your head	cm	cm	cm
Your height	cm	cm	cm
Around your waist	cm	cm	cm

F

1 Write who you think is taller, the policeman or the burglar.

2 Measure each person. Were you right?

A Find out the favourite colour of car of the children in your class.

Make up a table to show the information.

Draw a block graph to show the information.

Colour of car	red	black	
Number of cars		.	

Find out the favourite make of car of the children in your class.

Make up a table to show this information.

Show this information on a block graph.

Can you tell from your graphs if any child has chosen both the most popular make and the most popular colour?

B Find out from all of the children in your class their favourite playground game.

Make up a table to show your information.

Draw a block graph to show the children's favourite games.

If no ball games were allowed in the playground, how many children would not be able to play their favourite game?

If no running was allowed, how many children would not be able to play their favourite game?

chasing

football

netball

skipping

hopscotch

C Discover the favourite fruit of each person in your class.

Make up a table to show your information using a tally system.

Draw a picture graph to show your information.

Favourite fruit	apple	orange	pear
Number of children	ЦНТ I	III	

To save time use 1 fruit to stand for two children.

 means that 2 children have apples as their favourite fruit.

means that 1 child has chosen apples.

D Draw a picture graph to show the favourite sports of the children in your class.

Choose suitable pictures so that one symbol stands for four children.

For example: could be used to show that 3 children have chosen football.

Answer any questions you can. Leave those you cannot do.

How children in Class 6B come to school

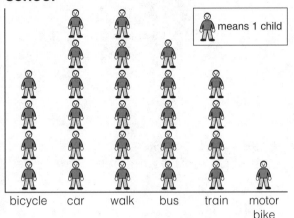

means 1 child

bicycle car walk bus train motor bike

1 How many children travel by train?

2 How many children travel by bicycle?

3 How many children walk to school?

4 How many children travel by car?

5 How many children either walk or cycle to school?

6 How many children travel by bus?

7 How many more children walk than arrive on a motorbike?

8 How many fewer children cycle to school than travel by car?

Playtime snacks

ytime snack	crisps	apples	drinks	biscuits
mber of children	JHT III	III	JHT I	JHT JHT I

9 How many children had crisps for their break?

10 How many children had biscuits for their break?

11 How many more children had a drink than had an apple?

Goal scorers for the school football team in 1997

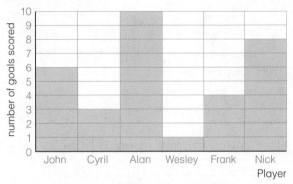

12 How many goals were scored by Alan?

13 How many more goals were scored by Nick than by Cyril?

14 How many fewer goals were scored by Wesley than by Alan?

15 How many goals were scored altogether by the team?

Goals scored for the school netball team in 1997

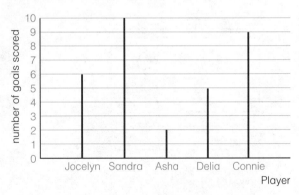

16 How many goals were scored by Sandra?

17 How many more goals than Asha did Connie score?

18 How many goals were scored altogether?

When you count coins, count the highest values first:

fifty pence
50p

50   ...70   ...80   ...85   ...87   ...88 pence.

A How much money in each box?

☆

50...60...70...75...77...78 pence

1

2

3

4

B Write words for ✱'s.
One 50p coin has the same value as:

☆ ✱ 10p coins   five

1 ✱ 1p coins   3 ✱ 2p coins

2 ✱ 5p coins

C

car   60p

spider   12p

skeleton   40p

snake   20p

lolly   10p

sweets   15p   FRUITIES

How much do you pay for:

☆ a skeleton and sweets? 40p+15p=55p

1 a car and a snake?

2 a lolly and a spider?

3 two snakes?

4 two lollies?

5 a snake and sweets?

D Which two coins will **exactly** pay for these?

☆ a spider   10p and 2p

1 a car   4 a lolly

2 a snake   5 a bag of sweets

3 a skeleton

Money

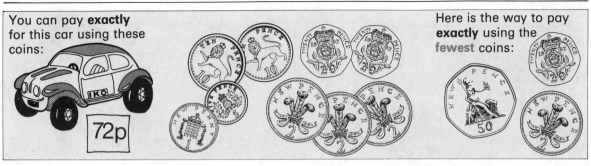

You can pay **exactly** for this car using these coins:

Here is the way to pay **exactly** using the **fewest** coins:

72p

Write a set of coins that will pay **exactly** for these:

☆ a soldier
27p   10p, 5p, 5p, 2p, 2p, 2p, 1p.

1 a monkey
45p

4 a gun
63p

2 a flying saucer
86p

5 a ship
57p

3 a doll
94p

6 a teddy bear
99p

Which two coins will pay **exactly** for these?

☆
BOOK of the WORLD   20p, 20p.
40p

1 ball
60p

4 cow
30p

2 pencil
11p

5 skipping rope
70p

3 lorry
55p

6 balloon
12p

C Write the fewest coins to pay **exactly** for:

☆ trick ink blot 72p   50p, 20p, 2p.

1 robot 48p

5 picture 99p

2 mug 62p

6 book 80p

3 bat 88p

7 sweets 55p

4 pen 75p

8 whistle 95p

D Write three coins to pay **exactly** for:

☆ cucumber 40p    20p, 10p, 10p.

1 apple
8p

5 orange
15p

2 carrots
26p

6 grapes
65p

3 melon
52p

7 pineapple
90p

4 onion
4p

8 grapefruit
16p

John buys a sweet for 6p.
He gives 10p to pay for it.
6p and **4p** make 10p.
He is given **4p** change.

Paula buys a cake for 34p.
She gives 50p to pay for it.
The baker gives change
using the fewest coins:

He says: '34 ...35 ...40 ...50'.
34p and **16p** make 50p.
Paula is given **16p change**.

A Write the missing amounts of money:

☆ Sally buys a chew for 3p.
She gives 5p to pay for it.
3p and ✳ make 5p.   **2p**
She is given ✳ change.   **2p**

1 Bill buys a bun for 7p.
He gives 10p to pay for it.
7p and ✳ make 10p.
He is given ✳ change.

2 Alan buys a sweet for 2p.
He gives 5p to pay for it.
2p and ✳ make 5p.
He is given ✳ change.

3 Jane buys a pencil for 5p.
She gives 10p to pay for it.
5p and ✳ make 10p.
She is given ✳ change.

4 Sue buys a flower for 14p.
She gives 20p to pay for it.
14p and ✳ make 20p.
She is given ✳ change.

B Copy and complete:

	cost	money given	change
☆	6p	10p	4p
1	3p	10p	
2	2p	5p	
3	18p	20p	
4	13p	20p	

C Write the coins that are added to these amounts to make 50p:

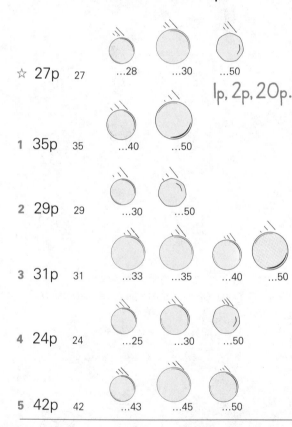

☆ 27p   27   ...28   ...30   ...50   **1p, 2p, 20p.**

1 35p   35   ...40   ...50

2 29p   29   ...30   ...50

3 31p   31   ...33   ...35   ...40   ...50

4 24p   24   ...25   ...30   ...50

5 42p   42   ...43   ...45   ...50

D Use coins if you need to.
How much **change** from 50p when you spend:

☆ 32p?   **18p**

1 46p?   5 36p?   9 22p?

2 44p?   6 30p?   10 19p?

3 40p?   7 25p?   11 16p?

4 39p?   8 28p?   12 11p?

Money

one pound coin

£1=100 pence

Mrs Black has spent 83p.
She gives the man a £1 coin.

The man gives change using the fewest coins.

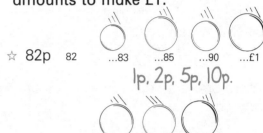

He says: '83 ...85 ...90 ...one pound'.

83p and 17p make one pound.
Mrs Black is given **17p change**.

Write words for ✳'s.
£1 has the same value as:

☆ ✳ 10p coins   ten

1 ✳ 50p coins   4 ✳ 1p coins

2 ✳ 5p coins   5 ✳ 2p coins

3 ✳ 20p coins

There is £1 in each of these boxes.
What is the hidden coin?

☆   1p

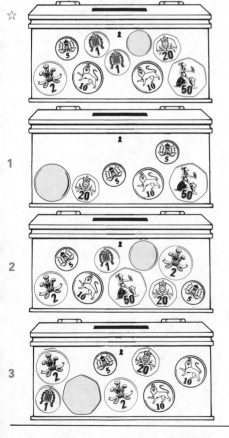

1

2

3

C Write the coins added to these amounts to make £1:

☆ 82p   82   ...83   ...85   ...90   ...£1

    1p, 2p, 5p, 10p.

1 86p   86   ...88   ...90   ...£1

2 73p   73   ...75   ...80   ...£1

3 68p   68   ...70   ...80   ...£1

4 57p   57   ...58   ...60   ...80   ...£1

D Use coins if you need to.
How much **change** from £1 when you spend:

☆ 54p?   46p

1 68p?   5 48p?   9 19p?

2 92p?   6 37p?   10 23p?

3 85p?   7 30p?   11 26p?

4 59p?   8 44p?   12 11p?

A Write down all of the different amounts you can pay using only two coins.

Write down all of the different amounts you can pay using only three coins.

Mrs. Patel buys some sweets. She pays the shopkeeper £1 and is given 2 coins in her change. Write down all of the different amounts that the sweets might have cost.

A chocolate machine takes only a £1 coin. It can give only 1 or 2 coins as change. Write down all of the different amounts that the machine can charge for chocolate.

What amounts could be charged if the machine was able to give 1, 2 or 3 coins as change?

Write down 4 coins that could be given as change from £1 when you spend:
1) 30p   2) 50p 3) 65p 4) 82p

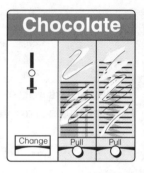

B There are three different groups of coins you can use to pay 4p.

Write down the 3 groups of coins.

How many different groups of coins can you find to pay 10p if you do not use any 1p coins?

How many different groups of coins can you find to pay 50p if you use only silver coins?

Using only 50p, 20p and 10p coins, how many different groups of coins can you find to pay a bill of £1?

Parking meters take only 50p, 20p, 10p and 5p coins.

How many different groups of coins can you find to pay for one hour's parking?

How many different groups of coins can you find to pay for 2 hour's parking if you have no 5p coins?

How many different groups of coins can you find to pay for 3 hour's parking if you have no 20p or 5p coins?

Hansley County Council
PARKING CHARGES
1 hour   35p
2 hours 80p
3 hours £1.30
Vehicles left longer than 3 hours will be clamped.

Answer any questions you can. Leave those you cannot do.

How much money is in each bag?

1

2

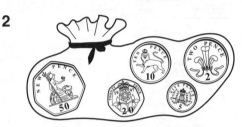

3

Write down two coins that together are worth:

4 15p

5 52p

6 £1.20

Write down 3 coins that together are worth:

7 31p

8 72p

9 £1.05

10 £1.60

If the fewest coins are used to pay these amounts exactly, which coins are used?

11 23p

12 38p

13 67p

14 96p

Write coins to pay exactly for:

15 a packet of crisps.

16 a pen.

17 a ball.

18 a puppet.

What is the cost of:

19 a packet of crisps and a pen?

20 a packet of mints and a ball?

21 a pen and a ball?

22 a puppet and a packet of crisps?

How much change will you receive when:

23 you give £1 to pay for a puppet?

24 you give 50p to pay for a packet of mints?

25 you give 50p to pay for a pen?

26 you give £1 to pay for a ball?

27 you give £1 to pay for a packet of mints?

What is the total cost for each of these snacks?

28 Soup 85p

Toast 25p

Ice cream ..50p

29 Beans on toast ..£1.55

Apple Pie £1.20

Coffee £0.80

Animals on the farm

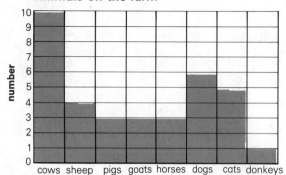

A Use the block graph to answer these:

1 How many sheep?
2 How many cows?
3 How many animals altogether?
4 How many more dogs than donkeys?
5 How many more cats than goats?
6 What is the difference between the number of pigs and the number of horses?
7 What is the difference between the number of cats and the number of cows?
8 What is the difference between the number of dogs and the number of goats?

B Copy and complete the table:

1 ——————————— 2 ———
3 ———————————————
4 ——— 5 —————
6 ———————————

line	estimate	measure	difference
1	cm	cm	cm
2	cm	cm	cm
3	cm	cm	cm
4	cm	cm	cm
5	cm	cm	cm
6	cm	cm	cm

C How much money in each box?

1

2

3

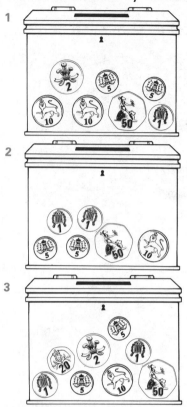

D Which 3 coins will exactly pay for these?

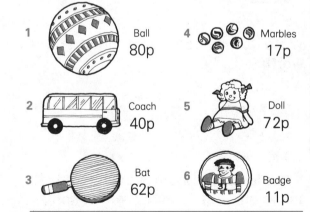

1 Ball 80p
2 Coach 40p
3 Bat 62p
4 Marbles 17p
5 Doll 72p
6 Badge 11p

E How much change from £1 when you spend:

1 75p? 4 59p? 7 32p?
2 86p? 5 52p? 8 25p?
3 63p? 6 71p? 9 18p?

These solid shapes are **cubes**:

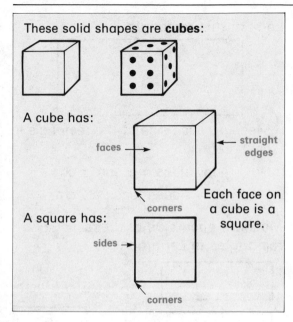

A cube has:

faces →

← straight edges

corners

Each face on a cube is a square.

A square has:

sides →

corners

A Use a cube if you need to.

1 How many faces on a cube?

2 How many straight edges on a cube?

3 How many corners on a cube?

4 How many sides on a square?

5 How many corners on a square?

B You need some squared paper.
Make a pattern of squares on your paper.

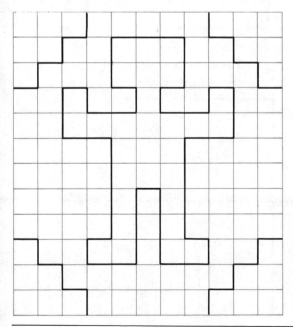

C

1 Measure each side of this square in centimetres.

2 Are all 4 sides the same length?

D Part of the square is hidden.
Write the length of each side:

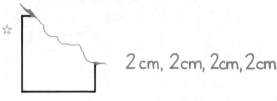

☆   2 cm, 2 cm, 2 cm, 2 cm

1

2

3

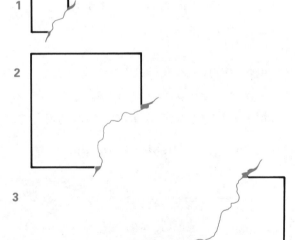

This solid shape is a **cuboid**.

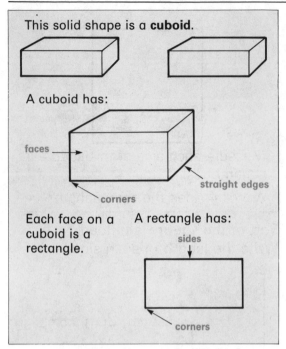

A cuboid has:

faces → straight edges

corners

Each face on a cuboid is a rectangle.

A rectangle has:

sides

corners

A Use a cuboid if you need to:

1 How many faces on a cuboid?

2 How many straight edges on a cuboid?

3 How many corners on a cuboid?

4 How many sides on a rectangle?

5 How many corners on a rectangle?

B Here are some useful cuboids:

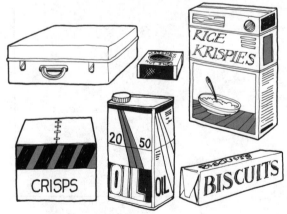

Name ten other useful cuboids.

☆ tea packet

C Look at this rectangle:

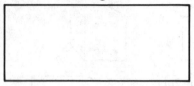

1 Measure each side of the rectangle in centimetres.

2 How many sides measure 5 cm?

3 How many sides measure 2 cm?

D Measure each side of these rectangles in centimetres:

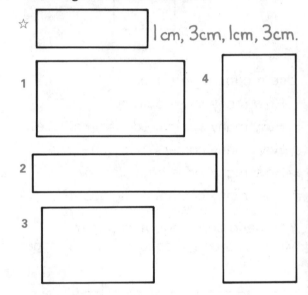

☆ 1 cm, 3 cm, 1 cm, 3 cm.

1

2

3

4

E Part of the rectangle is hidden. Write the length of each side:

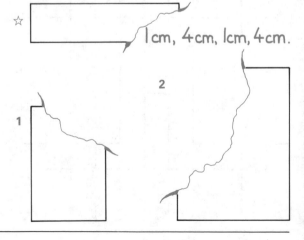

☆ 1 cm, 4 cm, 1 cm, 4 cm.

1

2

This solid shape is a **triangular prism**:

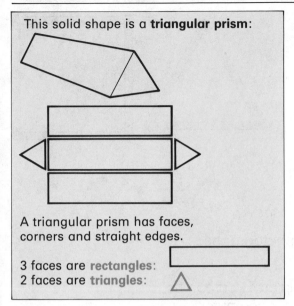

A triangular prism has faces, corners and straight edges.

3 faces are rectangles:
2 faces are triangles:

Use a triangular prism if you need to.

1 How many faces on a triangular prism?

2 How many straight edges on a triangular prism?

3 How many corners on a triangular prism?

4 How many sides on a triangle?

5 How many corners on a triangle?

B Where would you see these triangular prisms?

☆ on a house

1 TOBLERONE
2
3
4

C Triangles can be seen in many places:

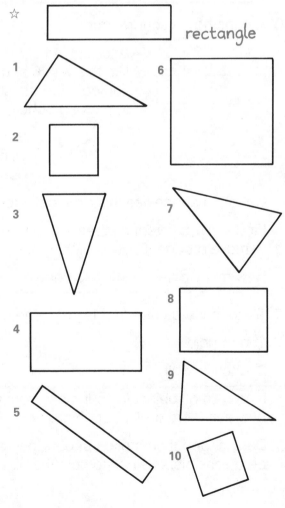

Draw five other pictures that show triangles.

D Write the name of each shape:

☆ rectangle

1
2
3
4
5
6
7
8
9
10

A Make a triangle and a square from plastic geo-strips.

Pick up each shape by a corner holding one in each hand.

What happens?

Which is the stronger shape?

Try to find some examples of this stronger shape in your school building.

Draw pictures to show where it has been used.

Try to find some examples of pictures or photographs showing this strong shape in use.

You may be able to find some more examples if you can use an encyclopaedia software program on your computer.

B A cube has 6 square faces.

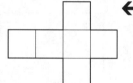

← After cutting out a shape like this with 6 squares, you can fold the shape to make a cube.

Here is another shape → with 6 squares that you can fold to make a cube.

Cut out a shape like this and fold it to form a cube.

Find some different shapes with 6 squares that you can fold to make a cube. Draw a picture of each of your shapes.

How many different shapes can you find?

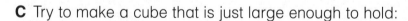

C Try to make a cube that is just large enough to hold:

1 a marble

2 a tennis ball

Find a small object in your classroom which is between 6 cm and 10 cm high.

Design, and then make out of paper, a cuboid which would be a sensible size box to hold the object.

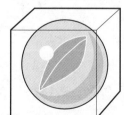
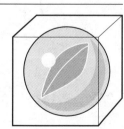

Answer any questions you can. Leave those you cannot do.

Name these solid shapes.

1   2   3

4 How many faces on a cuboid?

5 How many corners on a cuboid?

6 How many straight edges on a cuboid?

7 How many faces on a triangular prism?

8 How many corners on a triangular prism?

9 How many straight edges on a triangular prism?

10 What shape is each face on a cube?

11 What two different shapes would you find on the faces of a triangular prism?

Each square below has one red side, part of which is hidden. What is the length of the red side?

12

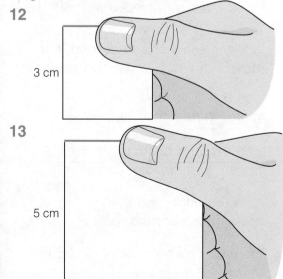

3 cm

13

5 cm

Each rectangle below has one red side, part of which is hidden. What is the length of the red side?

14

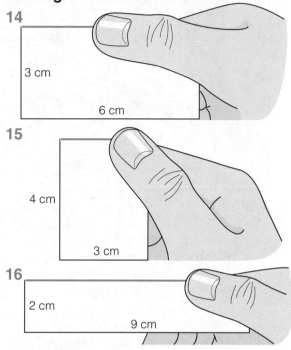

3 cm

6 cm

15

4 cm

3 cm

16

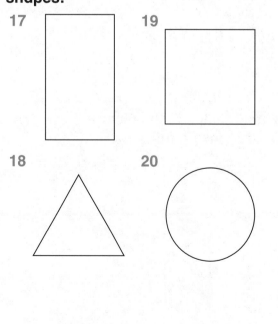

2 cm

9 cm

Write the name of each of these shapes:

17   19

18   20

A Write 15 things in the picture that turn.

☆  doorhandle

---

B Write 5 things in the picture that **can** make a **full** turn.

☆  wheel

---

C Write 5 things in the picture that **cannot** make a **full** turn.

☆  door

Turns can be made:

clockwise or **anti-clockwise**.

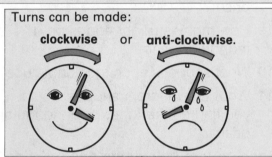

D What are you facing if you:

☆ face the door, and then *make* 1 *full turn clockwise?* the door

1 face the teacher's desk, and then *make* 1 *full turn anti-clockwise?*

2 face the door, and then *make* $\frac{1}{2}$ *turn clockwise?*

3 face the light switch, and then *make* $\frac{1}{2}$ *turn anti-clockwise?*

4 face the door, and then *make* $\frac{1}{4}$ *turn anti-clockwise?*

5 face the teacher's desk, and then *make* $\frac{1}{4}$ *turn clockwise?*

Angles

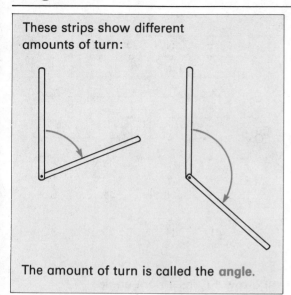

These strips show different amounts of turn:

The amount of turn is called the **angle**.

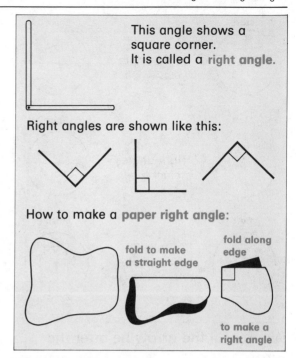

This angle shows a square corner.
It is called a **right angle**.

Right angles are shown like this:

How to make a **paper right angle**:

fold to make a straight edge

fold along edge

to make a right angle

A Which is the larger angle?
Write **black** or **red**:

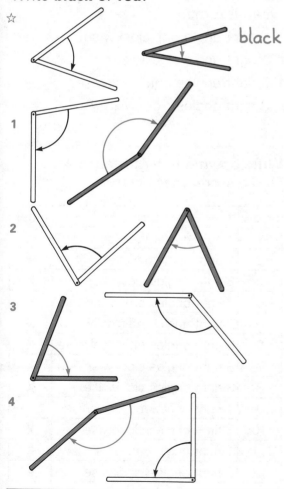

☆ black

1

2

3

4

B Make a paper right angle.
See pictures above.

C Use your paper right angle.
Are these angles right angles?

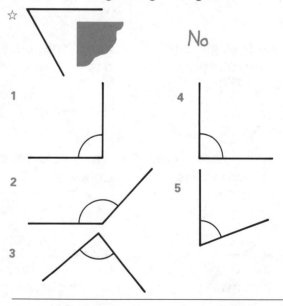

☆ No

1

4

2

5

3

D Use your paper right angle to find 20 right angles in your classroom.

☆ corner of the window frame

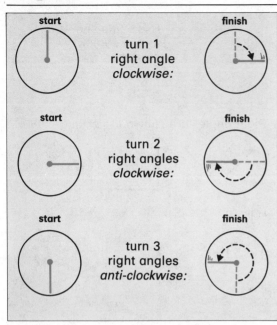

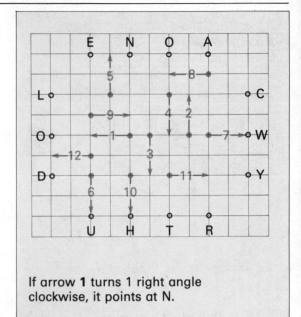

If arrow **1** turns 1 right angle clockwise, it points at N.

A Where will the arrow be after the turn?

☆ turn 2 right angles *clockwise*

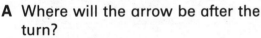

1 turn 1 right angle *anti-clockwise*

4 turn 1 right angle *anti-clockwise*

2 turn 2 right angles *anti-clockwise*

5 turn 3 right angles *clockwise*

3 turn 3 right angles *clockwise*

6 turn 3 right angles *anti-clockwise*

B At which letter will arrow 3 point when it turns:

☆ 1 right angle anti-clockwise? W

1 1 right angle clockwise?

2 3 right angles anti-clockwise?

3 3 right angles clockwise?

C Write down a letter for each ✳. Find a secret message:

arrow	turn	letter
☆ 1	1 right angle anti-clockwise	H
2	1 right angle anti-clockwise	✳
3	3 right angles clockwise	✳
4	2 right angles anti-clockwise	✳
5	1 right angle anti-clockwise	✳
6	3 right angles anti-clockwise	✳
7	3 right angles clockwise	✳
8	3 right angles clockwise	✳
9	1 right angle anti-clockwise	✳
10	3 right angles clockwise	✳
11	1 right angle anti-clockwise	✳
12	3 right angles clockwise	✳

Angles

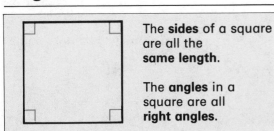

The **sides** of a square are all the **same length**.

The **angles** in a square are all **right angles**.

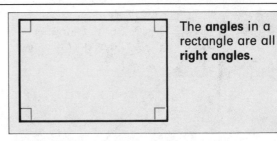

The **angles** in a rectangle are all **right angles**.

A Are these shapes squares?
Write **yes** or **no**:

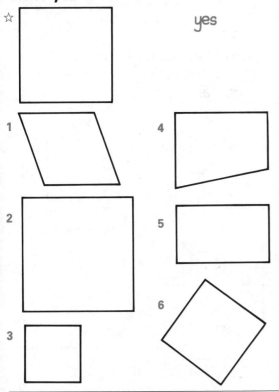

yes

C Are these shapes rectangles?
Write **yes** or **no**:

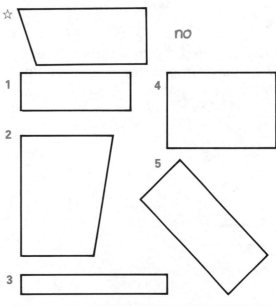

no

D Are the two **red** sides of these rectangles the same length?

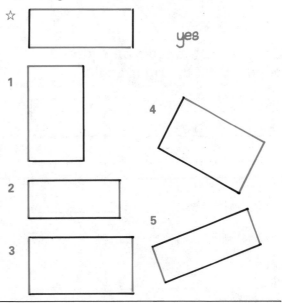

yes

B Why are these shapes **not** squares?

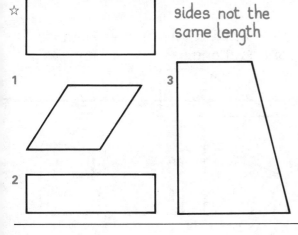

sides not the same length

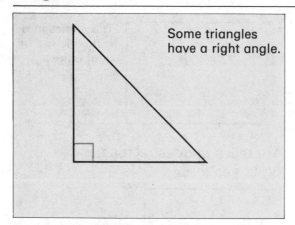

Some triangles have a right angle.

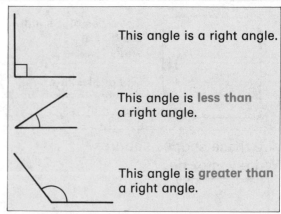

This angle is a right angle.

This angle is **less than** a right angle.

This angle is **greater than** a right angle.

A You will need a paper right angle. Do these triangles have right angles? Write **yes** or **no**:

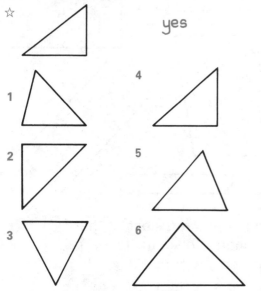

☆ yes

1

2

3

4

5

6

B Copy these triangles on squared paper. Mark the right angles:

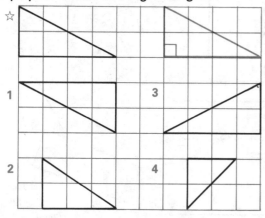

☆

1

2

3

4

C Are these angles right angles? If not, are they greater or less than right angles?

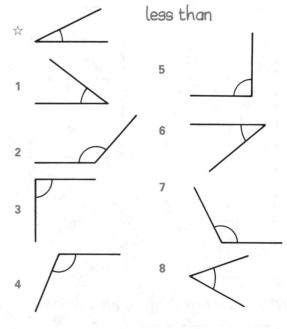

☆ less than

1

2

3

4

5

6

7

8

D How many angles in these shapes are right angles?

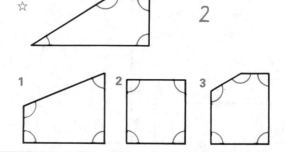

☆ 2

1

2

3

Name these solid shapes:

1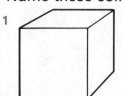

2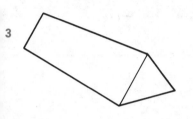

3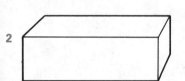

Name these shapes:

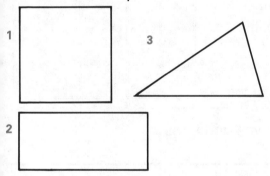

1

3

2

Part of each rectangle is hidden.
Write the length of each side:

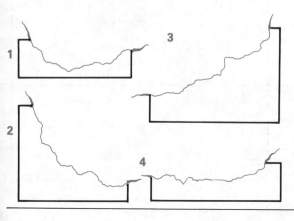

1

2

3

4

D Are these angles right angles?
Write **yes** or **no**:

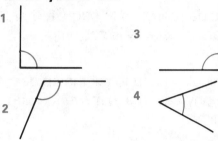

1

2

3

4

E Where will the arrow be after the turn?

1 turn 1
right angle
clockwise

3 turn 3
right angles
anti-clockwise

2 turn 2
right angles
anti-clockwise

4 turn 2
right angles
anti-clockwise

F How many:

1 squares?

2 rectangles?

3 triangles?

4 circles?

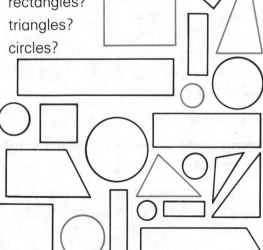

A Work out a set of instructions for this spider to escape from the maze.

The spider can turn through 1, 2 or 3 right angles clockwise or anti-clockwise.

You will also need to tell the spider how many squares to move forward each time.

Design a maze of your own on squared paper.

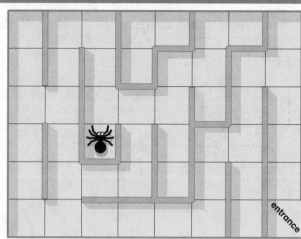

Work out a set of instructions which would lead to the centre of the maze from the entrance.

B The side of each small square on this window frame measures 10 cm.

← The fly walks up the frame from point A but will make only turns of 1 right angle clockwise. What is the shortest journey you can find so that the fly walks along every section of the frame?

Carry out the same investigation with these frames: →

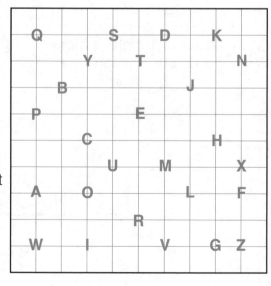

C On this grid you can spell out names with moves and turns.

For example: Start at B.

Move 3 sections towards the letter J, turn 1 right angle clockwise, move forward 1 section (letter E). Turn 1 right angle anti-clockwise, move 4 sections forward, turn 3 right angles clockwise, move forward 2 sections (letter N).

You have spelt out the name BEN.

Now work out some instructions to spell out your own name.

Can you work out a set of instructions to spell out your name using only clockwise turns?

Answer any questions you can. Leave those you cannot do.

Which is the larger angle, black or red?

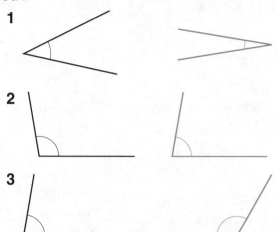

1

2

3

You need a paper right angle or a protractor. Say if each angle below is a right angle, smaller than a right angle or larger than a right angle.

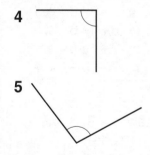

4

5

Draw a picture to show where each arrow will be after the turn.

6

turn 1 right angle anticlockwise.

7

turn 3 right angles clockwise.

How many right angles in:

8 a square?

9 a right-angled triangle?

10 a rectangle?

Say whether or not it is possible to draw:

11 a four-sided shape with 4 right angles.

12 a three-sided shape with 2 right angles.

13 a five-sided shape with 5 right angles.

14 a four-sided shape with 3 right angles and one angle smaller than a right angle.

15 a four-sided shape with 2 angles larger than right angles.

16 a three-sided shape with 2 angles larger than right angles.

17 a four-sided shape with 4 angles smaller than right angles.

18 a four-sided shape with 3 angles larger than right angles.

19 How many degrees are there in a right angle?

20 How many degrees in half a turn?

Are these angles acute or obtuse?

21

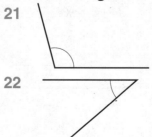

22

Are these angles acute or obtuse?

(23) 68°

(24) 123°

UNITS

	0	1	2	3	4	5	6	7	8	9
0	0	1	2	3	4	5	6	7	8	9
1	10	11	12	13	14	15	16	17	18	19
2	20	21	22	23	24	25	26	27	28	29
3	30	31	32	33	34	35	36	37	38	39
4	40	41	42	43	44	45	46	47	48	49
5	50	51	52	53	54	55	56	57	58	59
6	60	61	62	63	64	65	66	67	68	69
7	70	71	72	73	74	75	76	77	78	79
8	80	81	82	83	84	85	86	87	88	89
9	90	91	92	93	94	95	96	97	98	99

T E N S (row labels on left)

How many sweets altogether?

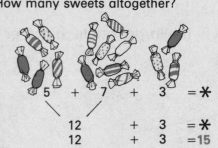

$$5 + 7 + 3 = *$$
$$12 + 3 = *$$
$$12 + 3 = 15$$

You can add the groups in a different order:

$7+5+3= *$ $3+5+7= *$
$12 + 3=$ $8 + 7= *$
$12 + 3=15$ $8 + 7=15$

The easiest order is to make 10 first:

$7+3+5= *$
$10 +5= *$
$10 +5=15$

A Use the number square if you need to. Write numbers for **∗**'s:

☆ $6+7= *$ 13

1 $7+6= *$ 6 $5+11= *$
2 $5+9= *$ 7 $11+5= *$
3 $9+5= *$ 8 $14+6= *$
4 $8+7= *$ 9 $6+14= *$
5 $7+8= *$

B Write numbers for **∗**'s:

☆ $6+5= *$ 11   5 $4+8= *$
1 $16+5= *$ 6 $14+8= *$
2 $26+5= *$ 7 $24+8= *$
3 $36+5= *$ 8 $34+8= *$
4 $46+5= *$ 9 $44+8= *$

C Write numbers for **∗**'s:

☆ $5+10= *$ 15   5 $7+20= *$
1 $15+10= *$ 6 $17+20= *$
2 $25+10= *$ 7 $27+20= *$
3 $35+10= *$ 8 $37+20= *$
4 $45+10= *$ 9 $47+20= *$

D Write numbers for **∗**'s:

☆ $6+5+4= *$ 15

1 $8+3+2= *$ 7 $7+2+8= *$
2 $7+5+5= *$ 8 $5+4+5= *$
3 $4+7+3= *$ 9 $2+9+8= *$
4 $9+2+1= *$ 10 $6+4+6= *$
5 $8+6+4= *$ 11 $7+4+6= *$
6 $6+3+4= *$ 12 $7+10+2= *$

E Answer these:

☆ With 3 darts Jim scores 8, 3 and 7. How many does he score altogether?   18

1 Jill spends 3p, 6p and 7p. How much does she spend altogether?

2 Jo has 4 marbles. He wins 5 and buys 6 more. How many marbles does he have altogether?

3 A dog makes 8 barks, 3 barks and 7 barks. How many barks altogether?

4 Fred saves 8p, 2p and 3p. How much does he save altogether?

5 With 3 darts Ann scores 6, 5 and 5. How many does she score altogether?

Add together 23 and 6:

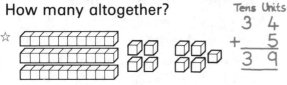

2 tens   **9 units**

Tens	Units
2	3
+	6
2	9

Martin has 24 stamps.
He is given 4 more stamps.
How many stamps does he
have altogether?

T	U
2	4
+	4
2	8

He has **28** stamps altogether.

How many altogether?

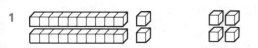

Tens	Units
3	4
+	5
3	9

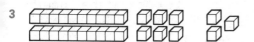

1

2

3

4

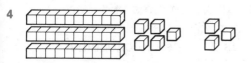

C Use addition to answer these:

☆ Ann has 12 books.
She buys 7 more.
How many books
does she have
altogether?

T	U
1	2
+	7
1	9

1 John has 2 mice. He buys 4 more.
How many mice does he have
altogether?

2 Joy has 16 stamps. She collects 3 more.
How many stamps does she have
altogether?

3 Jack has 24 fish. He catches 5 more.
How many fish does he have
altogether?

4 Jill has 52p. She is given 7p more.
How much does she have altogether?

Copy and complete:

☆
Tens	Units
5	2
+	6

Tens	Units
5	2
+	6
5	8

1
Tens	Units
2	6
+	3

3
Tens	Units
3	4
+	5

5
Tens	Units
4	2
+	6

2
Tens	Units
5	2
+	7

4
Tens	Units
2	5
+	3

6
Tens	Units
7	4
+	4

D Copy and complete:

☆
T	U
3	2
+	6

T	U
3	2
+	6
3	8

1
T	U
2	4
+	3

3
T	U
6	1
+	7

5
T	U
4	0
+	8

2
T	U
3	4
+	4

4
T	U
2	0
+	9

6
T	U
9	3
+	4

Add together 32 and 24:

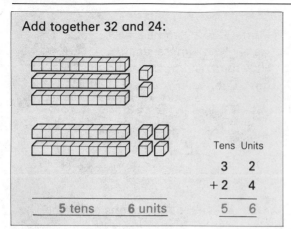

Tens	Units
3	2
+2	4

5 tens   6 units | 5 | 6 |

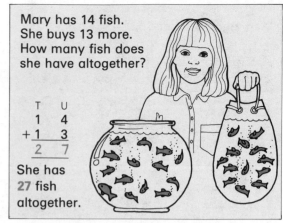

Mary has 14 fish.
She buys 13 more.
How many fish does
she have altogether?

T	U
1	4
+1	3
2	7

**She has
27 fish
altogether.**

A How many altogether?

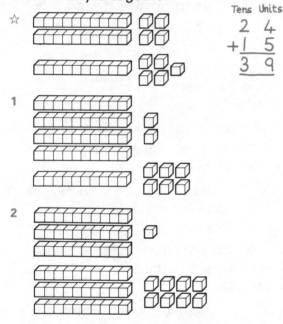

Tens	Units
2	4
+1	5
3	9

C Use addition to answer these:

☆ Mike has 25 marbles.
He wins 14 more.
How many marbles
does he have altogether?

T	U
2	5
+1	4
3	9

1 A garage has 36 cars. 13 more are brought in. How many cars in the garage altogether?

2 A dog eats 24 biscuits, and then 25 more. How many biscuits does the dog eat altogether?

3 Joy makes 34 skips and then another 44 skips. How many skips does she make altogether?

4 Jack runs 60 metres and then another 36 metres. How many metres does he run altogether?

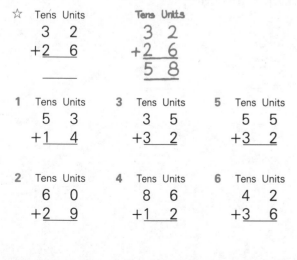

B Copy and complete:

☆
Tens	Units
3	2
+2	6
—	—

Tens	Units
3	2
+2	6
5	8

1
Tens	Units
5	3
+1	4

2
Tens	Units
6	0
+2	9

3
Tens	Units
3	5
+3	2

4
Tens	Units
8	6
+1	2

5
Tens	Units
5	5
+3	2

6
Tens	Units
4	2
+3	6

D Copy and complete:

☆
T	U
3	5
+4	2
—	—

T	U
3	5
+4	2
7	7

1
T	U
2	3
+3	5

2
T	U
4	4
+3	3

3
T	U
1	8
+6	1

4
T	U
2	7
+5	2

5
T	U
4	2
+3	7

6
T	U
6	6
+3	3

Tens and units

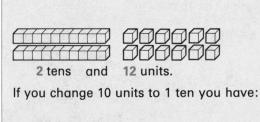

2 tens and 12 units.

If you change 10 units to 1 ten you have:

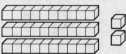

3 tens and 2 units.

So: 2 tens and 12 units
=3 tens and 2 units.

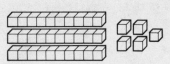

3 tens and 5 units.

If you change 1 ten to 10 units you have:

2 tens and 15 units.
So: 3 tens and 5 units
=2 tens and 15 units.

Use apparatus if you need to.
Change 10 units to 1 ten.
Write numbers for *'s:

☆ 3 tens 14 units=4 tens and 4 units

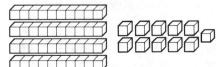

1 4 tens 11 units=* tens and * units

2 2 tens 16 units=* tens and * units

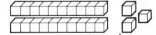

3 3 tens 13 units=* tens and * units

Change 10 units to 1 ten.
Write numbers for *'s:

☆ 4 tens and 16 units=5 tens and 6 units

1 1 ten and 15 units=* tens * units

2 3 tens and 18 units=* tens * units

3 6 tens and 14 units=* tens * units

4 5 tens and 17 units=* tens * units

5 2 tens and 19 units=* tens * units

C Use apparatus if you need to.
Change 1 ten to 10 units.
Write numbers for *'s:

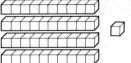

☆ 2 tens 3 units=1 ten and 13 units

1 4 tens 1 unit=* tens * units

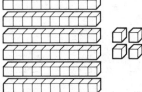

2 6 tens 4 units=* tens * units

3 3 tens 7 units=* tens * units

D Change 1 ten to 10 units.
Write numbers for *'s:

☆ 3 tens 8 units=2 tens and 18 units

1 2 tens 4 units=* ten * units

2 4 tens 2 units=* tens * units

3 7 tens 5 units=* tens * units

4 6 tens 2 units=* tens * units

5 5 tens 6 units=* tens * units

Add together 34 and 8:

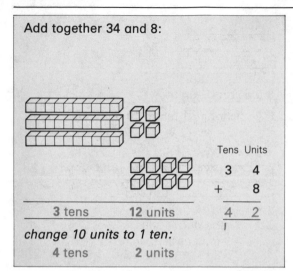

	Tens	Units
	3	4
+		8
	4	2
	₁	

3 tens | **12** units

change 10 units to 1 ten:

4 tens | **2** units

Trevor has 19 mice.
He buys 6 more.
How many mice does he have altogether?

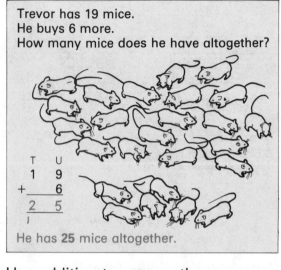

	T	U
	1	9
+		6
	2	5
	₁	

He has **25** mice altogether.

A How many altogether?

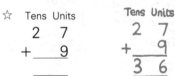

	Tens	Units
	2	3
+		9
	3	2

1

2

3

C Use addition to answer these:

☆ Jeff eats 27 nuts.
He then eats 5 more.
How many nuts does
he eat altogether?

	T	U
	2	7
+		5
	3	2

1 Tom has 7 sweets. He buys 6 more.
How many sweets does he have
altogether?

2 Beverley has 37 pence. She is given
5 pence more. How many
pence does she have altogether?

3 David has 38 pencils. He is given
7 more. How many pencils
does he have altogether?

B Copy and complete:

☆
Tens	Units
2	7
+	9

Tens	Units
2	7
+	9
3	6

1
Tens	Units
5	4
+	7

3
Tens	Units
4	7
+	8

5
Tens	Units
5	8
+	6

2
Tens	Units
6	5
+	6

4
Tens	Units
6	9
+	7

6
Tens	Units
7	5
+	9

D Copy and complete:

☆
T	U
3	5
+	7

T	U
3	5
+	7
4	2

1
T	U
4	7
+	8

3
T	U
5	6
+	5

5
T	U
8	2
+	8

2
T	U
6	3
+	9

4
T	U
4	7
+4	6

6
T	U
3	8
+	5

Add together 47 and 16:

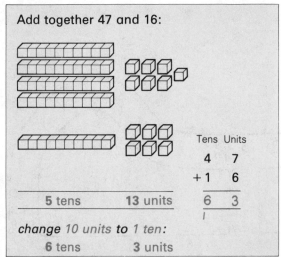

Tens	Units
4	7
+1	6
6	3

5 tens   13 units

change 10 units **to** 1 ten:
   6 tens   **3** units

How many altogether?

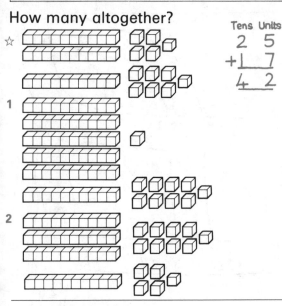

Tens Units
2	5
+1	7
4	2

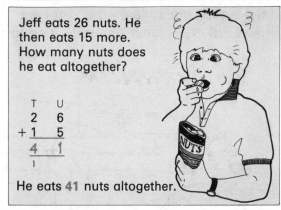

Jeff eats 26 nuts. He then eats 15 more. How many nuts does he eat altogether?

T	U
2	6
+1	5
4	1

He eats 41 nuts altogether.

C Use addition to answer these:

☆ David has 35 pencils. He is given 17 more. How many pencils does he have altogether?

T	U
3	5
+1	7
5	2

1 Sue has 37 sweets. She buys 18 more. How many sweets does she have altogether?

2 A donkey eats 29 carrots and then 14 more. How many carrots altogether?

3 Jack scores 43 and 49 at darts. How many did he score altogether?

4 In Class 3 there are 12 girls and 19 boys. How many children altogether?

5 A piece of wood is 38 cm long. A second piece is 27 cm long. How long are the two pieces together?

Copy and complete:

☆ Tens Units
6 4
+2 8

Tens Units
6 4
+2 8
9 2

1 Tens Units
3 5
+2 8

3 Tens Units
1 7
+5 8

5 Tens Units
5 4
+3 6

2 Tens Units
4 7
+3 9

4 Tens Units
6 9
+1 8

6 Tens Units
2 7
+2 7

D Copy and complete:

☆ T U
2 3
+3 8

T U
2 3
+3 8
6 1

1 T U
4 4
+4 7

3 T U
6 3
+2 7

5 T U
4 7
+3 7

2 T U
7 8
+1 9

4 T U
5 5
+2 7

6 T U
2 9
+6 6

If the police car follows the smallest
answer at each junction, who is caught?

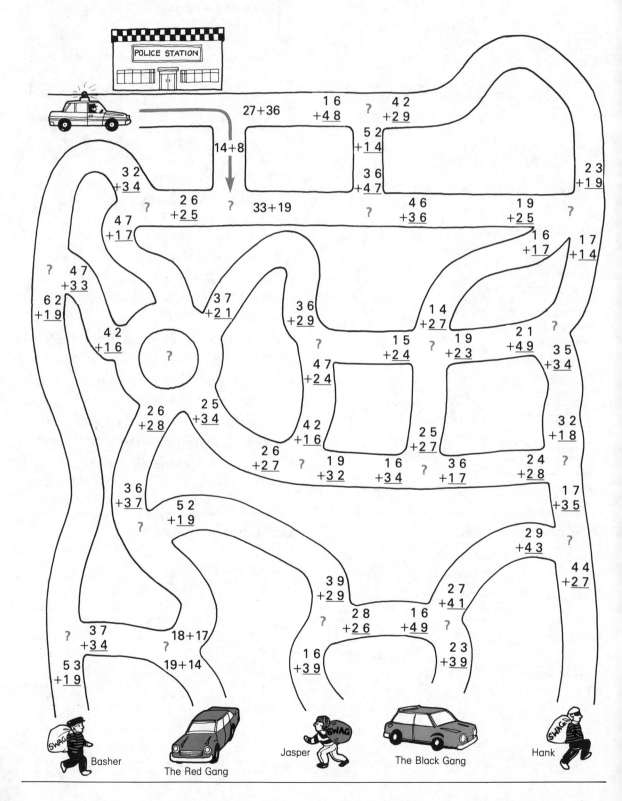

POLICE STATION

27+36

$\begin{array}{r} 1\ 6 \\ +4\ 8 \\ \hline \end{array}$?

$\begin{array}{r} 4\ 2 \\ +2\ 9 \\ \hline \end{array}$

$\begin{array}{r} 5\ 2 \\ +1\ 4 \\ \hline \end{array}$

14+8

$\begin{array}{r} 3\ 2 \\ +3\ 4 \\ \hline \end{array}$

$\begin{array}{r} 3\ 6 \\ +4\ 7 \\ \hline \end{array}$

$\begin{array}{r} 2\ 3 \\ +1\ 9 \\ \hline \end{array}$

? $\begin{array}{r} 2\ 6 \\ +2\ 5 \\ \hline \end{array}$? 33+19

$\begin{array}{r} 4\ 6 \\ +3\ 6 \\ \hline \end{array}$?

$\begin{array}{r} 1\ 9 \\ +2\ 5 \\ \hline \end{array}$?

$\begin{array}{r} 4\ 7 \\ +1\ 7 \\ \hline \end{array}$

$\begin{array}{r} 1\ 6 \\ +1\ 7 \\ \hline \end{array}$

$\begin{array}{r} 1\ 7 \\ +1\ 4 \\ \hline \end{array}$

? $\begin{array}{r} 4\ 7 \\ +3\ 3 \\ \hline \end{array}$

$\begin{array}{r} 6\ 2 \\ +1\ 9 \\ \hline \end{array}$

$\begin{array}{r} 3\ 7 \\ +2\ 1 \\ \hline \end{array}$

$\begin{array}{r} 3\ 6 \\ +2\ 9 \\ \hline \end{array}$

$\begin{array}{r} 1\ 4 \\ +2\ 7 \\ \hline \end{array}$

?

$\begin{array}{r} 4\ 2 \\ +1\ 6 \\ \hline \end{array}$

? $\begin{array}{r} 1\ 5 \\ +2\ 4 \\ \hline \end{array}$?

$\begin{array}{r} 1\ 9 \\ +2\ 3 \\ \hline \end{array}$

$\begin{array}{r} 2\ 1 \\ +4\ 9 \\ \hline \end{array}$?

$\begin{array}{r} 3\ 5 \\ +3\ 4 \\ \hline \end{array}$

?

$\begin{array}{r} 4\ 7 \\ +2\ 4 \\ \hline \end{array}$

$\begin{array}{r} 2\ 6 \\ +2\ 8 \\ \hline \end{array}$

$\begin{array}{r} 2\ 5 \\ +3\ 4 \\ \hline \end{array}$

$\begin{array}{r} 2\ 5 \\ +2\ 7 \\ \hline \end{array}$

$\begin{array}{r} 3\ 2 \\ +1\ 8 \\ \hline \end{array}$

$\begin{array}{r} 2\ 6 \\ +2\ 7 \\ \hline \end{array}$

?

$\begin{array}{r} 1\ 9 \\ +3\ 2 \\ \hline \end{array}$

$\begin{array}{r} 1\ 6 \\ +3\ 4 \\ \hline \end{array}$?

$\begin{array}{r} 3\ 6 \\ +1\ 7 \\ \hline \end{array}$

$\begin{array}{r} 2\ 4 \\ +2\ 8 \\ \hline \end{array}$?

$\begin{array}{r} 3\ 6 \\ +3\ 7 \\ \hline \end{array}$

$\begin{array}{r} 5\ 2 \\ +1\ 9 \\ \hline \end{array}$

$\begin{array}{r} 1\ 7 \\ +3\ 5 \\ \hline \end{array}$

?

$\begin{array}{r} 2\ 9 \\ +4\ 3 \\ \hline \end{array}$?

$\begin{array}{r} 4\ 4 \\ +2\ 7 \\ \hline \end{array}$

$\begin{array}{r} 3\ 9 \\ +2\ 9 \\ \hline \end{array}$

$\begin{array}{r} 2\ 7 \\ +4\ 1 \\ \hline \end{array}$

?

$\begin{array}{r} 2\ 8 \\ +2\ 6 \\ \hline \end{array}$

$\begin{array}{r} 1\ 6 \\ +4\ 9 \\ \hline \end{array}$?

? $\begin{array}{r} 3\ 7 \\ +3\ 4 \\ \hline \end{array}$ 18+17 ?

$\begin{array}{r} 5\ 3 \\ +1\ 9 \\ \hline \end{array}$ 19+14

$\begin{array}{r} 1\ 6 \\ +3\ 9 \\ \hline \end{array}$

$\begin{array}{r} 2\ 3 \\ +3\ 9 \\ \hline \end{array}$

Basher

The Red Gang

Jasper   SWAG

The Black Gang

Hank   SWAG

A

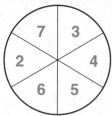

Work out all of the different totals you could score with 2 darts on this darts board. (Both darts must score)

How many different ways can you find to score 15 with 3 darts?

A red ring is now added to the outside of the board. A dart landing in this ring scores double. For example, the dart shown would score 6.

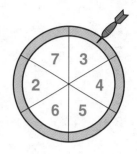

How many different totals can you score with 2 darts on this new board?

How many different ways can you find to score 15 on this new board with 3 darts?

What is the smallest number of darts you would need to score a) 50?   b) 99?   c) 101?

B

5	18	4	16
12	7	1	14
20	8	11	3
9	2	6	15

Make this playing board using thin card. Each side of the board should measure 40 cm.

You will need 3 large counters for each player.

Place the playing board on the floor and mark a throwing line about 1 metre away from the board.

Players take turns to throw all 3 counters trying to land them on the board.

Scores are made by taking the highest numbered square the counter is touching. For example, the counter in this picture would score 20......

| 12 | 7 |
| 20 | 8 |

Players add their scores until one player scores 100 or more. This player is the winner.

(Calculators are not allowed)

Can you make the game more exciting by redesigning the board?

For example, you might allow larger spaces for smaller numbers.

Answer any questions you can. Leave those you cannot do.

You should not use a calculator for any questions on this page.

Write numbers for $*$'s

1 9 + 6 = $*$

2 12 + 7 = $*$

3 5 + 9 + 4 = $*$

4 22 + 7 = $*$

5 48 + 20 = $*$

6 84 + 9 = $*$

7 36 + $*$ = 41

8 98 + 5 = $*$

9 86 + 20 = $*$

10 65 + $*$ = 95

Copy and complete:

11
```
  5 3
+   6
```

12
```
  6 2
+1 4
```

13
```
  2 8
+   7
```

14
```
  4 3
+3 8
```

15
```
  6 4
+2 9
```

Use addition to answer these:

16 Sita has 5 magazines. She collects 7 more. How many does she have altogether?

17 Jonathan has 15 football cards. If he collects 6 more, how many has he altogether?

18 Joshua has 62p. If he is given another 35p, how much money does he have altogether?

19 Anish scores 38 in a darts game. If he scores 55 on his second throw, what is his total score?

20 Mr. Jacobs spends £84 on a radio and £48 on a pair of shoes. How much does he spend altogether?

21 In 3 journeys a bus carried 36 passengers, 28 passengers and 38 passengers. How many passengers did the bus carry altogether?

Write numbers for $*$s

22 109 + 6 = $*$

23 310 + $*$ = 318

24 435 + $*$ = 455

25 217 + 9 = $*$

Copy and complete:

26
```
  2 1 5
+4 2 3
```

27
```
  2 6 7
+5 1 8
```

28
```
  3 7 4
+1 6 9
```

(29)
```
  1 5 2 6
+3 1 4 2
```

(30)
```
  2 3 4 5
+2 3 4 6
```

(31)
```
  1 8 9 2
+3 0 2 9
```

Subtraction

0	1	2	3	4	5	6	7	8	9
10	11	12	13	14	15	16	17	18	19
20	21	22	23	24	25	26	27	28	29
30	31	32	33	34	35	36	37	38	39
40	41	42	43	44	45	46	47	48	49
50	51	52	53	54	55	56	57	58	59
60	61	62	63	64	65	66	67	68	69
70	71	72	73	74	75	76	77	78	79
80	81	82	83	84	85	86	87	88	89
90	91	92	93	94	95	96	97	98	99

Use the number square if you need to.
Write numbers for *'s:

☆ $10-8=$ * 2   6 $12-4=$ *
1 $10-7=$ *   7 $12-5=$ *
2 $10-6=$ *   8 $12-6=$ *
3 $10-5=$ *   9 $12-7=$ *
4 $10-4=$ *   10 $12-8=$ *
5 $10-3=$ *   11 $12-9=$ *

Write numbers for *'s:

☆ $6-4=$ * 2   6 $9-2=$ *
1 $16-4=$ *   7 $19-2=$ *
2 $26-4=$ *   8 $29-2=$ *
3 $36-4=$ *   9 $39-2=$ *
4 $46-4=$ *   10 $49-2=$ *
5 $56-4=$ *   11 $59-2=$ *

Write numbers for *'s:

☆ $17-10=$ * 7   6 $92-10=$ *
1 $27-10=$ *   7 $92-20=$ *
2 $37-10=$ *   8 $92-30=$ *
3 $47-10=$ *   9 $92-40=$ *
4 $57-10=$ *   10 $92-50=$ *
5 $67-10=$ *   11 $92-60=$ *

D Use subtraction to find the **difference** between:

☆ 9 and 3 6   6 4 and 14
1 10 and 3   7 4 and 15
2 11 and 3   8 4 and 16
3 12 and 3   9 4 and 17
4 13 and 3   10 4 and 18
5 14 and 3   11 4 and 19

E Use **subtraction** to answer these:

☆ There are 19 flowers in a garden.
8 are picked. How many are left? ||

1 A piece of spaghetti
is 18 cm long.
Lucy eats 7 cm.
What length is left?

2 There are 16 cars in a garage. 5 are
sold. How many are left?

3 Mandy has 19 sweets. She eats 9.
How many has she left?

4 A spider catches 16 flies. It eats 7.
How many are left?

F Use **subtraction** to answer these:

☆ Mary is 9. Her brother is 18. How
many years difference in their ages?
q

1 The score in a
football match was
Reds 6 Greens 8.
What was the
difference in scores?

SCORE BOARD

REDS 6

GREENS 8

2 A circus has 18 dogs and 4 horses.
How many more dogs than horses?

3 Jack is 8 and Ben is 14. How many
years difference in their ages?

4 A shop has 20 blue cases and 7 red
cases. How many more blue cases
than red cases?

From 36 subtract 4:

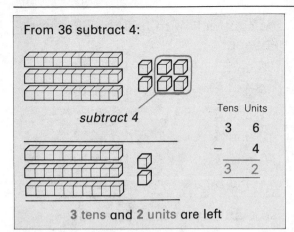

subtract 4

	Tens	Units
	3	6
−		4
	3	2

3 tens and **2** units are left

A How many are left when you subtract 5 from each group:

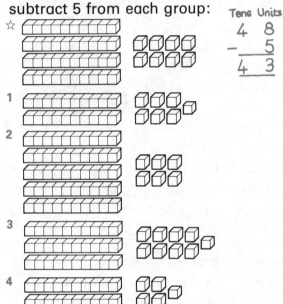

☆

	Tens	Units
	4	8
−		5
	4	3

1

2

3

4

B Copy and complete:

☆

Tens	Units
3	8
	− 6

Tens	Units
3	8
	− 6
3	2

1

Tens	Units
4	5
	− 4

2

Tens	Units
3	9
	− 7

3

Tens	Units
2	4
	− 3

4

Tens	Units
9	5
	− 5

5

Tens	Units
6	8
	− 7

6

Tens	Units
5	7
	− 5

C Use **subtraction** to answer these. Find how many left if:

☆ Bill has 15 frogs and 3 get away.

	T	U
	1	5
−		3
	1	2

1 Trevor has 47 marbles and loses 6.

2 Dan has 56 stamps and gives away 5.

3 Sam has 25 chips and eats 4.

4 Denise has 19 balloons and 7 burst.

5 Anna has 28 sweets and eats 7.

6 Paul has 37 crisps and eats 6.

7 Ann has 69 books and gives away 6.

8 Jo has 77 comics and gives away 7.

D Use subtraction to answer these. What is the **difference** in ages if:

	T	U
	2	9
−		7
	2	2

☆ Sally is 7 and her mother is 29?

1 Lucy is 6 and her father is 38?

2 Ann is 5 and her father is 29?

3 Jack is 19 and Jim is 8?

4 Sally is 17 and Alice is 7?

5 Jenny is 8 and her mother is 29?

6 Mr Brown is 36 and his son is 4?

7 Sharon is 2 and her father is 26?

8 John is 7 and his mother is 28?

E Copy and complete:

☆

T	U
5	7
	− 4

T	U
5	7
	− 4
5	3

1

T	U
3	5
	− 3

2

T	U
5	9
	− 7

3

T	U
7	5.
	− 4

4

T	U
5	8
	− 5

5

T	U
2	9
	− 6

6

T	U
7	8
	− 4

Subtraction

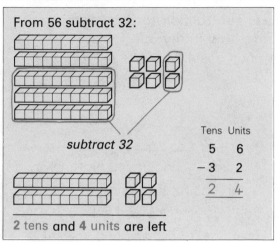

From 56 subtract 32:

subtract 32

Tens	Units
5	6
−3	2
2	4

2 tens and **4 units** are left

How many are left when you
subtract 13 from each group:

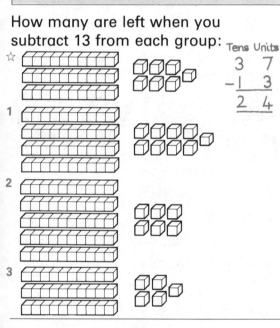

Tens	Units
3	7
−1	3
2	4

☆

1

2

3

Copy and complete:

☆
Tens	Units
4	5
−2	3

Tens	Units
4	5
−2	3
2	2

1
Tens	Units
6	9
−2	6

3
Tens	Units
7	9
−2	4

5
Tens	Units
6	9
−4	7

2
Tens	Units
5	4
−3	1

4
Tens	Units
9	4
−7	2

6
Tens	Units
8	9
−5	0

C Use subtraction to answer these:

☆ **Find how many left if:**
there are 37 birds
on a branch and
14 fly away.

T	U
3	7
−1	4
2	3

1 A dog has 49 biscuits and eats 27.

2 Bill has 59 coins and gives away 18.

3 Alan has 36 marbles and loses 24.

4 A rose has 24 petals and 10 fall off.

5 A bird catches 27 worms and eats 14.

D These are the scores in a darts game:

SCORE BOARD	
JOHN	58
MARY	24
PAUL	35
SHARON	89
BILL	47

Use subtraction to
find the difference
in scores between:

T	U
5	8
−2	4
3	4

☆ Mary and John

1 John and Paul   5 Mary and Paul

2 Paul and Sharon   6 Bill and Sharon

3 Sharon and Mary   7 John and Sharon

4 Mary and Bill   8 Bill and John

E Copy and complete:

☆
T	U
4	9
−3	2

T	U
4	9
−3	2
1	7

1
T	U
3	7
−1	4

3
T	U
9	6
−3	5

5
T	U
5	7
−2	7

2
T	U
5	9
−2	2

4
T	U
8	4
−3	3

6
T	U
9	6
−1	1

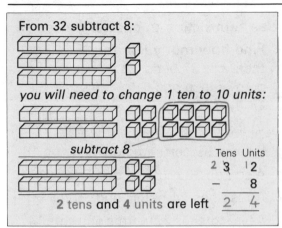

From 32 subtract 8:

you will need to change 1 ten to 10 units:

subtract 8

	Tens	Units
	2 3̶	¹2
−		8
	2	4

2 tens and **4** units are left   2 4

A How many left in each group when
you subtract 7:

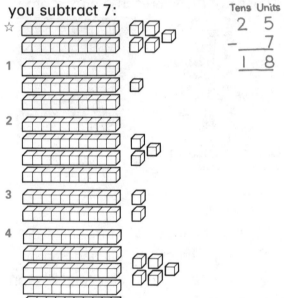

	Tens	Units
☆		2 5
−		7
		1 8

B Copy and complete:

☆	Tens	Units
	5	6
−		9

	Tens	Units
	5	6
−		9
	4	7

1

	Tens	Units
	4	1
−		6

2

	Tens	Units
	3	6
−		8

3

	Tens	Units
	3	5
−		8

4

	Tens	Units
	2	2
−		9

5

	Tens	Units
	6	2
−		4

6

	Tens	Units
	4	0
−		4

C Use subtraction to answer these.
Find how many left if:

☆ John has 42 stamps
and gives away 9.

	T	U
	4	2
−		9
	3	3

1 Ann has 27 books and gives away 8.

2 Sarah has 32 toys and gives away 9.

3 Bob has 21 mice and sells 6.

4 Tom has 30 stamps and loses 4.

5 Jill has 24 dolls and gives away 7.

D Use subtraction to find the difference
between the number of:

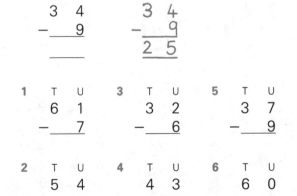

WE'VE GOT
9 LIONS, 24 ELEPHANTS
6 TIGERS, 43 MONKEYS
8 CAMELS, 35 FLAMINGOS

☆ lions and flamingos

1 monkeys and tigers

2 tigers and elephants

3 camels and flamingos

4 elephants and lions

5 camels and monkeys

6 elephants and camels

	T	U
	3	5
−		9
	2	6

E Copy and complete:

☆	T	U
	3	4
−		9

	T	U
	3	4
−		9
	2	5

1

	T	U
	6	1
−		7

2

	T	U
	5	4
−		8

3

	T	U
	3	2
−		6

4

	T	U
	4	3
−		5

5

	T	U
	3	7
−		9

6

	T	U
	6	0
−		7

Subtraction

From 35 subtract 17:

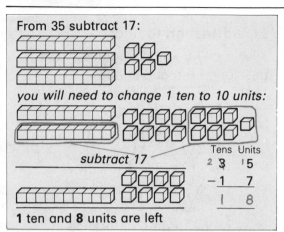

you will need to change 1 ten to 10 units:

subtract 17

	Tens	Units
	²3	¹5
−	1	7
	1	8

1 ten and **8** units are left

How many left in each group when you subtract 19:

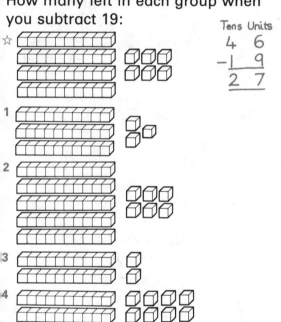

	Tens	Units
☆	4	6
−	1	9
	2	7

1

2

3

4

Copy and complete:

☆
	Tens	Units
	3	3
−	1	5

	T	U
	3	3
−	1	5
	1	8

1
	Tens	Units
	4	2
−	1	7

2
	Tens	Units
	3	5
−	1	6

3
	Tens	Units
	2	1
−	1	8

4
	Tens	Units
	5	4
−	2	8

5
	Tens	Units
	6	2
−	3	7

6
	Tens	Units
	8	4
−	6	7

C Use subtraction to answer these.

Find how many pence left if:

	T	U
	3	2
−	1	4
	1	8

☆ John has 32p and spends 14p.   18p left

1 Sally has 51p and spends 16p.

2 Jill has 37p and spends 28p.

3 Bob has 64p and spends 38p.

4 Sharon has 76p and spends 57p

5 Jack has 82p and spends 43p.

D

vase	bicycle	chair	picture	lamp
£28	£71	£47	£39	£19

Use subtraction to answer these.

How many pounds difference in cost between:

	T	U
	4	7
−	2	8
	1	9

☆ a vase and a chair?

1 a lamp and a chair?   £19 difference

2 a picture and a chair?

3 a picture and a bicycle?

4 a chair and a bicycle?

5 a vase and a bicycle?

6 a lamp and a vase?

E Copy and complete:

☆
	T	U
	4	2
−	1	6

	T	U
	4	2
−	1	6
	2	6

1
	T	U
	3	1
−	1	7

2
	T	U
	4	2
−	2	3

3
	T	U
	6	3
−	3	8

4
	T	U
	8	6
−	2	9

5
	T	U
	9	6
−	5	8

6
	T	U
	7	0
−	3	4

A Use **addition** to find:

☆ the number of loaves altogether.

```
  T  U
  4  8
+ 2  4
  7  2
```

48 loaves 24 loaves

1 The number of toys altogether.

39 toys 46 toys

2 The number of fish altogether.

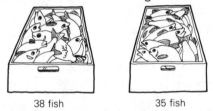

38 fish 35 fish

3 The number of pies altogether.

45 pies 37 pies

4 The number of leaves altogether.

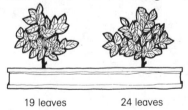

19 leaves 24 leaves

5 The number of flowers altogether.

26 flowers 54 flowers

B Use **subtraction** to find:

☆ how many years difference in age between Fred and Jane?

```
  T  U
  2  0
-    7
  1  3
```

Fred Jane

1 How many metres difference in length between rope A and rope B?

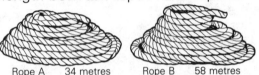

Rope A 34 metres Rope B 58 metres

2 The difference in pounds between Mike's money and Sally's money?

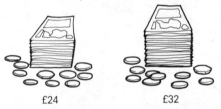

£24 £32

3 How many apples are left when 24 are taken from this box:

60 apples

4 The length of string left when 35 centimetres are cut off?

length of string: 82 centimetres

5 How much is left if you have 92p but spend 48p?

Revision for pages 82–94

Copy and complete:

	T U		T U		T U
1	2 3 +4 5	4	4 7 +4 2	7	2 3 +4 2
2	3 2 +5 7	5	1 3 +3 6	8	5 5 +4 4
3	2 3 +7 6	6	4 4 +3 2	9	6 3 +2 5

B Use addition to answer these:

1 Mike has 15 marbles. He wins 14 more. How many marbles does he have altogether?
2 Mary has 23 pence. She is given 28 pence more. How much does she have altogether?
3 Bill walks 39 metres and then another 46 metres. How many metres does he walk altogether?
4 There are 26 fish in a tank. 7 more are put in. How many fish in the tank altogether?
5 Jill has 29 toys. She is given 12 more. How many toys does she have altogether?

D Copy and complete:

	T U		T U		T U
1	9 4 −2 3	3	4 7 −2 5	5	9 3 −2 3
2	6 8 −2 7	4	6 4 −3 3	6	8 7 −6 4

E Use subtraction to answer these. How many left if:

1 John has 16 balloons and 7 burst.
2 Anna has 36 crisps and eats 9.
3 Jill has 44 coins and gives away 15.
4 There are 58 straws in a box and 12 are used.
5 Ben has 41 mice and sells 26.
6 35 people are on a bus and 17 get off.
7 Mrs James bakes 43 cakes and 27 are eaten.
8 Kate has 32 sweets and gives away 18.
9 A book shop has 53 comics and 19 are sold.
10 A clown has 76 balloons and gives away 48.
11 There are 52 children in the Hall and 17 leave.

C Copy and complete:

	T U		T U		T U
1	4 3 − 8	3	6 1 − 9	5	5 3 − 6
2	3 4 − 7	4	7 2 − 5	6	4 1 − 3

F Copy and complete:

	T U		T U		T U
1	6 1 −2 9	3	7 3 −3 7	5	3 0 −1 7
2	5 4 −3 6	4	6 2 −2 6	6	6 0 −1 9

Find the number that falls into each bucket:

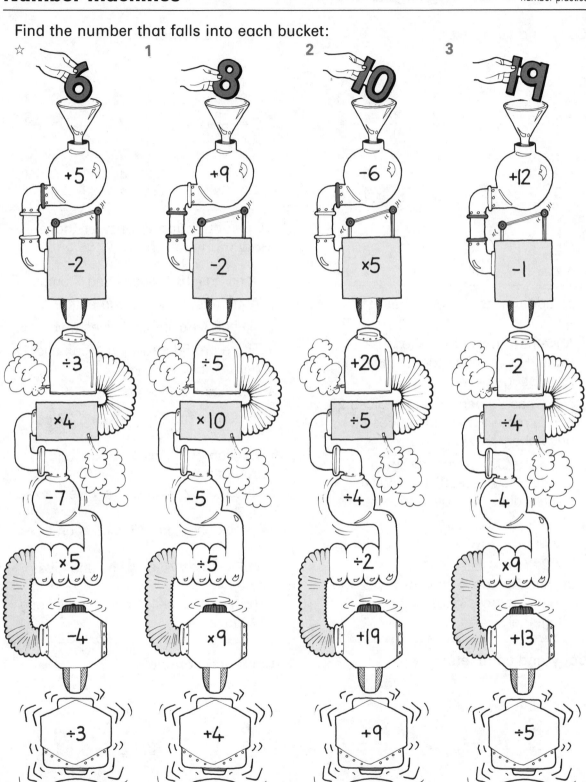

A This stepping stone picture shows ➜ how to work out the difference between 28 and 71.

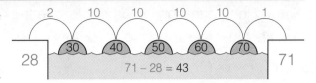

Stepping stones can only be used for the 'tens' numbers.

Explain how the stepping stone system works. ➜

What question does this stepping stone picture help you to answer?

Answer this question by using the stepping stone method.
74 – 26 = *

Answer this question using the stepping stone method but without drawing a diagram:

58 – 19 = *

Try to answer this question using the stepping stone method but in your head: **62 – 35 = ***

Make up some more difficult questions for yourself and try to answer them in your head.

B Using only the figures **5** and **7** and the **minus sign** this calculator display can be taken back to zero.

`6` `4` `–` `7` `–` `7` `–` `7` `–` `7` `–` `7` `–` `7` `–` `5` `–` `5` `–` `5` `–`

Check this by pressing these keys on a calculator:
Here is a quicker way

`6` `4` `–` `5` `7` `–` `7` `–`

Can you take a calculator display back to zero when:

1 the display shows **32** and you can use only the keys **6, 4** and the **minus sign**?

2 the display shows **82** and you can use only the keys **8, 3** and the **minus sign**?

3 the display shows **43** and you can use only the keys **2, 7** and the **minus sign**?

4 the display shows **84** and you can use only the keys **5, 9** and the **minus sign**?

Answer any questions you can. Leave those you cannot do.

You should not use a calculator for any questions on this page.

Write numbers for ✱'s

1 9 − 5 = ✱

2 13 − 7 = ✱

3 36 − 4 = ✱

4 59 − ✱ = 53

5 65 − 5 = ✱

6 41 − 17 = ✱

7 54 − 18 = ✱

8 52 − ✱ = 35

9 86 − ✱ = 59

10 64 − ✱ = 24

11 99 − ✱ = 9

Copy and complete:

12
```
  4 5
−   3
```

13
```
  6 6
− 2 5
```

14
```
  3 7
−   9
```

15
```
  4 2
− 1 7
```

16
```
  7 3
− 2 8
```

Use subtraction to answer these:

17 Jamie has 8 badges. He gives away 3. How many does he have left?

18 Miranda has 16 sweets. She gives away 8. How many does she have left?

19 Anish has 46p. He spends 5p. How much money does he have left?

20 A baker bakes 74 loaves. After he has sold 19 loaves, how many does he have left?

21 If Alice is 18 and her mother is 43, what is the difference between their ages?

22 In a cricket match Rahul scores 93 runs and Tom scores 37 runs. What is the difference between their scores?

Write numbers for ✱'s

23 106 − 9 = ✱

24 332 − 30 = ✱

25 436 − 212 = ✱

26 99 − ✱ = 9

Copy and complete:

27
```
  4 8 5
− 2 1 3
```

28
```
  9 2 7
− 1 0 8
```

29
```
  4 2 7
− 1 4 5
```

30
```
  8 6 2
− 1 8 9
```

31
```
  2 6 3 9
− 1 4 1 8
```

32
```
  3 2 7 6
− 1 1 8 7
```

The beads on this necklace make a pattern.

The colour of the next bead would be red.

A In these necklace patterns, what colour is the next bead?

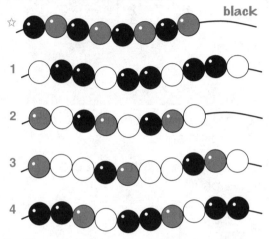

black

1

2

3

4

B What animal comes next in these patterns?

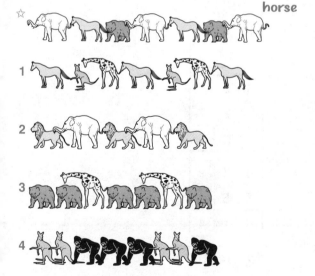

horse

1

2

3

4

5

On a hundred square grid a pattern like this ...

... looks like this when complete.

C Copy and complete these patterns on your own hundred square grid:

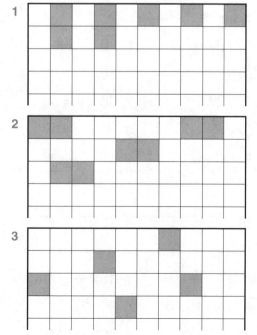

1

2

3

To complete a pattern first work out how the pattern is made.

1 3 4 6 7 9 10
  +2 +1 +2 +1 +2 +1

You can then find any missing numbers

A Copy and complete these patterns:

☆ 4 8 12 16 20 24 ✷

4 8 12 16 20 24 28

1 3 6 9 12 15 18 ✷

2 20 30 40 ✷ 60 70 80

3 5 ✷ 15 20 ✷ 30 35

4 2 4 ✷ ✷ 10 12 14

5 1 3 5 ✷ 9 ✷ 13

6 2 5 7 10 12 15 ✷

7 0 2 6 8 12 ✷ 18

8 0 3 8 ✷ 16 19 24

9 90 80 ✷ 60 50 ✷ 30

10 99 ✷ 95 ✷ 91 89 87

B Write numbers for ✷'s

☆ 26+9 = ✷ 35   5 86−7 = ✷

1 26+19 = ✷   6 86−17 = ✷

2 26+29 = ✷   7 86−✷ = 59

3 26+✷ = 65   8 ✷−37 = 49

4 ✷+49 = 75   9 86−47 = ✷

C Write numbers for ✷'s

☆ 28÷✷ = 7 4   5 10×5 = ✷

1 24÷4 = ✷   6 ✷×4 = 40

2 20÷4 = ✷   7 10×✷ = 30

3 ✷÷4 = 4   8 ✷×2 = 20

4 12÷4 = ✷   9 10×✷ = 10

In a magic square the numbers add up to the same total in all directions.

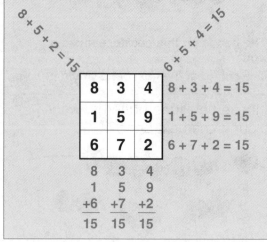

8+5+2 = 15   6+5+4 = 15

8	3	4	8 + 3 + 4 = 15
1	5	9	1 + 5 + 9 = 15
6	7	2	6 + 7 + 2 = 15

8 3 4
1 5 9
+6 +7 +2
15 15 15

D What are the numbers missing from these magic squares?

You may find it helpful to use a calculator.

☆
7	8	3
2		10
9	4	5
6

1
10	3	11
9	8	7
5	13	

2
10	5	
11	9	7
6	13	8

3
6	7	2
1	5	
8		4

4
1	14	15	4
12	7	6	9
8	11	10	
13		3	16

Number

Professor Muddleup has designed an electronic calculator but it does not work very well. The number keys light up but sometimes they show letters instead of numbers

A Use the clues below to work out the number value of each letter. Use a calculator to check your answer.

☆ $15 - E = 9$ $E = 6$

1 $11 + C = 20$

2 $51 - B = 43$

3 $15 \div G = 5$

4 $F + 55 = 57$

5 $A + 15 = 22$

6 $55 - 51 = D$

B Josie has been using Professor Muddleup's calculator.

Use the information she has found to work out the number value of each letter below.

☆ $A + A = 16$ $A = 8$

1 $12 - B = 7$

2 $36 \div 4 = C$

3 $40 - D = 38$

4 $E \times 9 = 27$

5 $24 - F = 24$

6 $8 \times G = 32$

7 $95 - H = 88$

8 $45 \div J = 9$

C Max has covered the signs on his calculator with coloured dots.

☆ Which sign is under the red dot if
$4 ● 8 = 12$? +

1 Which sign is under the white dot if $20 ○ 4 = 16$?

2 Which sign is under the black dot if $9 ● 5 = 45$?

Some of the number magnets do not work very well on the magnetic board and the numbers slip to the bottom.

D Rewrite each of these additions and subtractions with the correct answer.

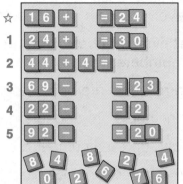

$16 + 8 = 24$

E Rewrite each of these multiplications with the correct answer.

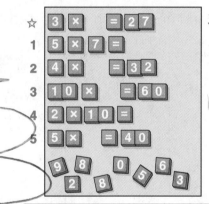

$3 \times 9 = 27$

F Rewrite each of these divisions with the correct answer.

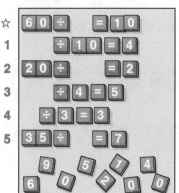

$60 \div 6 = 10$

A Are multiples of 2... odd numbers, even numbers or both odd and even numbers?

Are multiples of 5... odd numbers, even numbers or both odd and even numbers?

Use a calculator to investigate the multiples of five other numbers. In each case say if the multiples are odd numbers, even numbers or both odd and even numbers.

Do you get even numbers, odd numbers or both odd and even numbers when:

1 two even numbers are added together?

2 two odd numbers are added together?

3 an odd and an even number are added together?

4 two even numbers are multiplied together?

5 two odd numbers are multiplied together?

6 an odd and an even number are multiplied together?

B Copy this grid and write in numbers to complete it.

	odd numbers	multiples of 4	numbers less than 20
multiples of 5	25		15
numbers greater than 20		28	
multiples of 3	27		3

Every number in the first column must be odd.

Every number in the third row must be a multiple of 3, and so on.

Now complete this grid.

Try not to use the same number twice.

Make a grid of your own with four rows and four columns.

Write in sixteen numbers to complete your grid.

	even numbers	numbers larger than 40	multiples of 10
multiples of 2			
numbers greater than 25			
numbers between 30 and 50			

Answer any questions you can. Leave those you cannot do.

Continue these patterns to find:

1 which animal comes next.

2 which shape is next.

3 the colour of shirt the next ice skater is wearing.

4 The colour of the next hat.

What is the missing number in each of these patterns?

5 2 4 6 8 10 ✳

6 5 10 15 20 25 ✳

7 10 20 30 40 ✳ 60

8 4 ✳ 12 16 20 24

9 12 14 ✳ 18 20 22

10 30 27 24 21 18 ✳

11 60 50 40 ✳ 20 10

12 0 4 6 10 12 16 ✳

13 91 ✳ 87 85 83 81

14 40 38 35 33 30 28 ✳

Write numbers for ✳'s

15 14 + ✳ = 22

16 24 − ✳ = 6

17 9 × 4 = ✳

18 ✳ ÷ 3 = 10

19 8 + 5 = 5 + ✳

20 18 + 9 = 9 + ✳

21 24 + 35 = 50 + ✳

22 45 + 32 = 40 + 30 + ✳ + 2

23 5 × 10 = 10 × ✳

24 4 + 4 + 4 + 4 + 4 = 4 × ✳

Write down the value of each letter below:

25 A + 5 = 6

26 9 + B = 18

27 C + C = 20

28 D × 6 = 24

29 E ÷ 8 = 3

30 F + F + F = 12

31 G × G = 25

32 21 ÷ H = 7

What is the missing number in each pattern?

33 5 10 20 40 80 ✳

34 240 120 60 30 ✳

35 850 900 950 1000 ✳ 1100

36 1200 600 ✳ 150 75

Work out the missing number in each of these:

37
```
  2 3
+ 1 ✳
  3 6
```

38
```
  4 5
− ✳ 3
  1 2
```

39
```
  2 ✳ 4
×     5
1 3 2 0
```

40
```
    9 7
4 ) 3 8 ✳
```

A 1 How many bunches of 10 flowers can you make from 83 flowers?

2 $6 + * = 14$

3 $28 - 6 = *$

4 How many wheels on 7 cars?

5 Is 89 an odd number or an even number?

6 Which has the larger capacity, a teaspoon or a drinking glass?

7 Does a tennis ball weigh more or less than 1 kg?

8 How many centimetres in $\frac{1}{2}$ metre?

B 1 How much is left when Joe has 23p and spends 9p?

2 $24 + 15 = *$

3 $43 - 7 = *$

4 How many legs on 10 elephants?

5 How many each if 5 people have an equal share of 30 sweets?

6 What time is $\frac{1}{2}$ hour later than 2 o'clock?

7 How much is left if you have 50p and spend 27p?

8 How many faces on a cuboid?

C 1 $68 + * = 98$

2 $31 - 18 = *$

3 $3 \times 5 = *$

4 How many packs when 24 pies are packed in fours?

5 What time is $\frac{1}{2}$ hour earlier than $\frac{1}{4}$ to 5?

6 How much is left if you have £1 and spend 44p?

7 Is a chair heavier or lighter than 1 kg?

8 If you are facing North and turn through 2 right angles clockwise, which direction will you be facing?

D 1 $36 + 18 = *$

2 $48 - 35 = *$

3 $4 \times 6 = *$

4 $35 \div 5 = *$

5 Write down 2 coins that together are worth 70p.

6 What time is a quarter of an hour later than half past nine?

7 Which has the greater weight, a toothbrush or an apple?

8 How many right angles in a rectangle?

E 1 $13 + 48 = *$

2 $52 - 47 = *$

3 $5 \times 9 = *$

4 $24 \div 3 = *$

5 What is the fewest number of coins you can use to pay 86p?

6 Do you weigh more or less than 5 kg?

7 What time is $\frac{1}{4}$ hour earlier than 1 o'clock?

8 How many faces on a triangular prism?

F 1 $7 + 6 + 8 = *$

2 Billy is 16 and his father is 45. What is the difference between their ages?

3 $4 \times 8 = *$

4 $32 \div 4 = *$

5 What is the value of A if $A \times 9 = 36$?

6 Which has the smaller capacity, a bath or a dustbin?

7 How many $\frac{1}{4}$ l measures are needed to fill a 5 l bucket?

8 How many centimetres in $\frac{1}{4}$ metre?

A 1 9 + ✱ = 17

2 54 − 6 = ✱

3 How many odd numbers are there between 20 and 30?

4 How many legs on 7 horses?

5 Which is the longer distance, 1 metre or 99 cm?

6 Which is the heavier weight, 896 grams or 1 kg?

7 How many corners on a triangular prism?

B 1 36 + 25 = ✱

2 5 × 6 = ✱

3 If you have 53p and spend 28p, how much have you left?

4 What time is half an hour earlier than 12 o'clock?

5 What length of string would you need to form a square with sides of 10 cm?

6 How many is $\frac{1}{2}$ of 30?

7 What fraction of this square is red?

C 1 ✱ + 12 = 41

2 How many is 16 less than 54?

3 4 × 9 = ✱

4 80 ÷ 10 = ✱

5 How many whole oranges will give you 20 quarters?

6 Which two coins can you use to pay 30p?

7 If you are facing east and turn 1 right angle clockwise, which direction will you be facing?

D 1 4 × ✱ = 28

2 How many 5 cm lengths of string can be cut from a 35 cm length?

3 How much change from 50p when you spend 28p?

4 How many each if 40 flies are shared equally among 5 spiders?

5 How many centimetres in $1\frac{1}{2}$ metres?

6 What is the difference in age if Jason is 27 and Jane is 18?

E 1 What is the missing sign?
24 ✱ 8 = 16

2 How many toes on 7 feet?

3 How many groups of 4 can be made from 36?

4 What fraction of this triangle is black?

5 Which 3 coins can you use to pay 56p?

6 How many right angles in a square?

F 1 What is the difference between 6 and 19?

2 3 × 9 = ✱

3 Apples are packed in fives. How many packs can be made with 40 apples?

4 How much change from £1 when you spend 64p?

5 Two lengths of wood placed end to end measure 1 m. If 1 piece measures 65 cm what is the length of the other piece?

6 1 × 1 = ✱

A 1 $* + 9 = 15$

2 What number must you subtract from 20 to leave 12?

3 John is 17 and his grandmother is 82. What is the difference between their ages?

4 What is the missing number in this pattern? **15 25 $*$ 45 55**

5 $5 \times 8 = *$

6 $* \div 10 = 7$

7 Four children are given an equal share of £1. How much does each child receive?

B 1 $8 + * = 31$

2 $91 - 33 = *$

3 What is the largest odd number less than 100?

4 $10 \times 9 = *$

5 If $45 \div L = 9$, what is the value of L?

6 How many whole oranges do you need to make 20 halves?

7 What number of 5p coins have the same value as 50p?

C 1 $20 + 9 + 17 = *$

2 Joe has 4 coins. He has 77p altogether. Two of the coins are 20p and 5p. What are the other 2 coins?

3 Pencils are put into packs of 10. How many pencils are left over when 98 are packed?

4 $* \times 9 = 36$

5 $5 \div 5 = *$

6 If $18 + B = 30$, what is the value of B?

7 $80 - 18 = *$

D 1 $36 + * = 52$

2 $46 - 17 = *$

3 If you give £1 for 2 comics costing 22p each, how much change do you receive?

4 $* \div 4 = 7$

5 What time is $1\frac{1}{2}$ hours later than half past five?

6 Which 3 coins can you use to pay for a toy costing 71p?

7 If $92 - K = 71$, what is the value of K?

E 1 $59 + 40 = *$

2 $78 - 35 = *$

3 What is the number missing from this pattern? **98 78 58 38 $*$**

4 $3 \times * = 24$

5 $21 \div * = 7$

6 What fraction of this rectangle is coloured black?

7 How much change do you receive from £1 when you spend 42p?

F 1 Write down 5 coins that have a total value of 49p.

2 Is the height of your classroom door more or less than $1\frac{1}{2}$ metres?

3 $* \times 7 = 35$

4 $* \div 4 = 9$

5 How many whole apples do you need to make 24 quarters?

6 What time is $1\frac{1}{4}$ hours earlier than $\frac{1}{4}$ to 7?

7 If $Z \times 7 = 35$, what is the value of Z?